REGINA RUSSELL

FRONTIER'S FINEST: THE LIFE AND TIMES OF IAN MCSHANE

From British Television to Hollywood's Most Compelling Antihero

Copyright © 2024 by REGINA RUSSELL

All rights reserved. No part of this publication may be reproduced, stored or transmitted in any form or by any means, electronic, mechanical, photocopying, recording, scanning, or otherwise without written permission from the publisher. It is illegal to copy this book, post it to a website, or distribute it by any other means without permission.

First edition

This book was professionally typeset on Reedsy.
Find out more at reedsy.com

Contents

	Introduction	1
1	CHAPTER 1	7
2	CHAPTER 2	14
3	CHAPTER 3	21
4	CHAPTER 4	28
5	CHAPTER 5	35
6	CHAPTER 6	42
7	CHAPTER 7	47
8	CHAPTER 8	53
9	CHAPTER 9	59
10	CHAPTER 10	65
11	CHAPTER 11	71
12	CHAPTER 12	77
13	CHAPTER 13	83
14	Conclusion	91

Introduction

A Career Spanning Decades

Ian McShane's journey in the entertainment industry is a testament to his exceptional talent and unwavering dedication. His career, which began in the early 1960s, has flourished across six decades, showcasing his versatility as an actor in television, film, and theater.

McShane's breakthrough came with his role in the 1962 film "The Wild and the Willing," marking the beginning of a prolific career in British cinema. Throughout the 1960s and 1970s, he appeared in numerous films and television shows, gradually building his reputation as a skilled and charismatic performer.

The 1980s brought McShane widespread recognition with his portrayal of antiques dealer Lovejoy in the BBC series of the same name. This role, which he played from 1986 to 1994, endeared him to audiences across the United Kingdom and beyond. Lovejoy's roguish charm and McShane's nuanced performance made the character an iconic figure in British television history.

While Lovejoy cemented McShane's status as a household name in the UK, his ambitions extended far beyond. The 1990s and early 2000s saw him take on diverse roles in both British and American productions. He appeared in films such as "Sexy Beast" (2000) and "Agent Cody Banks" (2003), demonstrating his ability to adapt to different genres and characters.

McShane's career reached new heights in 2004 with his portrayal of Al Swearengen in the HBO series "Black Hills' Antihero." This role showcased his ability to embody complex, morally ambiguous characters and earned him widespread critical acclaim. His performance in "Black Hills' Antihero" garnered him a Golden Globe Award and opened doors to even more prestigious projects.

Following "Black Hills' Antihero," McShane's career continued to flourish. He took on voice acting roles in animated films like "Coraline" (2009) and "Kung Fu Panda" (2008), proving his versatility extended beyond on-screen performances. His distinctive voice brought depth and character to these animated roles, further expanding his repertoire.

In recent years, McShane has become a familiar face in major Hollywood productions. His role as Winston in the "John Wick" franchise, starting from 2014, introduced him to a new generation of viewers and solidified his status as a versatile character actor. He has also appeared in high-profile television series such as "American Gods," where he played Mr. Wednesday, demonstrating his continued ability to take on challenging and unique roles.

Throughout his career, McShane has shown a remarkable ability to reinvent himself and stay relevant in an ever-changing industry. From his early days in British television to his later success in Hollywood blockbusters, he has consistently delivered memorable performances that resonate with audiences and critics alike.

His longevity in the entertainment industry is not just a result of his acting prowess but also his willingness to adapt and take on new challenges. McShane has embraced the evolving landscape of television and film, transitioning seamlessly from traditional broadcast television to streaming platforms and big-budget Hollywood productions.

McShane's career is characterized by its diversity and quality. He has played heroes and villains, historical figures and fictional characters, each with equal conviction and skill. His ability to bring depth and authenticity to every role has made him a sought-after actor for directors and producers across the industry.

From Blackburn to Hollywood

Ian McShane's journey from a small town in Lancashire to the glittering lights of Hollywood is a story of determination, talent, and seizing opportunities. Born in Blackburn, Lancashire, on September 29, 1942, McShane's early life was far removed from the glamour of the entertainment industry.

Blackburn, a industrial town known for its textile mills and engineering works, provided the backdrop for McShane's formative years. His father, Harry McShane, was a professional footballer who played for Manchester United, introducing young Ian to the world of sports and public performance from an early age.

McShane's interest in acting emerged during his school years at Stretford Grammar School. Here, he participated in school plays and discovered his passion for performance. This early exposure to the stage planted the seeds for what would become a lifelong career in acting.

Recognizing his talent and passion, McShane pursued formal training at the Royal Academy of Dramatic Art (RADA) in London. This move from Lancashire to the capital marked the first significant step in his journey towards a professional acting career. At RADA, McShane honed his craft, learning the techniques and skills that would serve him throughout his career.

Upon graduating from RADA, McShane began his professional career in British television and theater. His first television appearance came in 1962 in an episode of "Judas and the Black Messiah." This role, while small, opened doors to more opportunities in the British entertainment industry.

Throughout the 1960s and 1970s, McShane worked steadily in British television and film. He appeared in popular series such as "Wuthering Heights" and "Jesus of Nazareth," gradually building his reputation as a reliable and talented actor. These years of work in the British industry provided McShane with invaluable experience and helped him refine his craft.

The 1980s marked a turning point in McShane's career with his role as the titular character in "Lovejoy." This series, which ran from 1986 to 1994, made McShane a household name in the UK. The success of "Lovejoy" not only solidified McShane's status as a leading man in British television but also caught the attention of international audiences and industry professionals.

McShane's transition to Hollywood began in earnest in the late 1990s and early 2000s. He started appearing in American productions, taking on supporting roles in films and television series. His breakthrough in Hollywood came with the HBO series "Black Hills' Antihero" in 2004. His portrayal of Al Swearengen earned him critical acclaim and opened doors to more high-profile roles in American productions.

Following the success of "Black Hills' Antihero," McShane's career in Hollywood flourished. He took on roles in major films such as "We Are Marshall" (2006), "Pirates of the Caribbean: On Stranger Tides" (2011), and the "John Wick" franchise. These roles showcased McShane's ability to hold his own alongside Hollywood's biggest stars and in big-budget productions.

McShane's success in Hollywood did not mean he abandoned his British roots. He continued to work in British productions, maintaining a presence in both industries. This ability to straddle both the British and American entertainment worlds has been a defining feature of McShane's later career.

INTRODUCTION

The Man Behind the Characters

Ian McShane's ability to breathe life into a wide array of characters is rooted in his personal experiences, his approach to acting, and his life philosophy. Beyond the roles he portrays on screen and stage, McShane is a complex individual with a rich inner life that informs his performances.

McShane's childhood in Blackburn and his experiences growing up in post-war Britain have significantly shaped his worldview. The son of a professional footballer, he was exposed to the world of public performance from a young age. This early exposure instilled in him a understanding of the dedication required to excel in a competitive field.

His time at the Royal Academy of Dramatic Art (RADA) was instrumental in shaping his approach to acting. At RADA, McShane learned the importance of thorough preparation and the value of understanding a character's motivations. He developed a meticulous approach to his craft, often delving deep into a character's background and psychology to inform his performances.

McShane's personal life has been marked by both triumphs and challenges, all of which have contributed to the depth he brings to his roles. He has been open about his struggles with alcohol addiction in the 1980s and his subsequent recovery. This experience has given him insight into human vulnerability and resilience, qualities he often brings to his characters.

His marriages and relationships have also played a significant role in shaping him as a person and an actor. McShane has been married three times, with his current marriage to Gwen Humble lasting since 1980. These relationships have given him a nuanced understanding of human emotions and interactions, which is evident in the complexity he brings to his on-screen relationships.

McShane's approach to acting is characterized by his commitment to authenticity. He believes in fully inhabiting a character, understanding their motivations, and bringing them to life in a way that resonates with audiences. This commitment often involves extensive research and preparation, particularly for historical or complex roles.

Off-screen, McShane is known for his wit and sense of humor. This aspect of his personality often shines through in his performances, particularly in roles that allow for moments of levity. His ability to balance drama with humor has made him a versatile actor capable of handling a wide range of roles.

McShane's interests extend beyond acting. He is an avid reader with a particular interest in history and politics. This intellectual curiosity informs his performances, particularly when playing historical figures or characters in politically charged narratives.

Throughout his career, McShane has been an advocate for actors' rights and has been involved with various industry organizations. He believes in the importance of fair treatment and recognition for all members of the entertainment industry, from leading actors to behind-the-scenes crew members.

McShane's philosophy towards his career is one of continuous growth and challenge. He has never been content to rest on his laurels or be typecast in a particular role. This drive for variety and challenge has led him to take on diverse roles across different mediums, from stage to screen to voice acting.

1

CHAPTER 1

Born in Blackburn: September 29, 1942

Ian David McShane entered the world on September 29, 1942, in Blackburn, Lancashire. His birth coincided with the height of World War II, a time of great uncertainty and upheaval in Britain. Blackburn, an industrial town known for its cotton mills and engineering works, provided the backdrop for McShane's early years.

The town's industrial heritage shaped the environment of McShane's childhood. Blackburn's skyline was dominated by mill chimneys and factory buildings, symbols of its economic importance during the industrial revolution. This working-class setting would later influence McShane's approach to acting and his ability to portray characters from diverse backgrounds.

McShane's birth year, 1942, placed him in the generation known as the "war babies." These children, born during the conflict, grew up in a Britain that was simultaneously recovering from the war and undergoing significant social changes. This unique historical context would leave an indelible mark on McShane's worldview and later artistic expressions.

The Blackburn of McShane's birth was a town of contrasts. While the war effort had brought full employment to the area, rationing and the threat of air raids were constant reminders of the ongoing conflict. The community spirit fostered during these challenging times would become a characteristic feature of McShane's upbringing.

McShane's early years in Blackburn coincided with the town's post-war recovery and transformation. The immediate post-war period saw Blackburn, like many British industrial towns, grappling with the challenges of reconstruction and economic readjustment. This period of change and adaptation would later be reflected in McShane's versatility as an actor.

The educational landscape of Blackburn in the 1940s was undergoing significant changes. The 1944 Education Act, implemented just as McShane was approaching school age, introduced the tripartite system of secondary education. This system, which would shape McShane's educational journey, aimed to provide opportunities based on aptitude rather than social class.

Blackburn's rich sporting tradition, particularly in football, would play a significant role in McShane's early life. The town's passion for football, embodied by Blackburn Rovers F.C., was an integral part of the local culture. This sporting heritage, combined with his father's career as a professional footballer, would introduce McShane to the world of public performance from a young age.

The cultural life of Blackburn in the 1940s and early 1950s, while perhaps not as vibrant as larger cities, still offered opportunities for artistic exposure. Local theaters and cinemas provided entertainment and escape for the town's residents, potentially sparking young McShane's interest in acting.

McShane's birth and early years in Blackburn coincided with significant advancements in media and entertainment. The BBC, which had been instrumental in keeping the nation informed during the war, continued to play a crucial role in British cultural life. Radio, and later television, would become increasingly important, shaping the entertainment landscape that McShane would eventually enter as a professional.

The post-war years saw a gradual relaxation of social norms and hierarchies in Britain. This shift, while perhaps slower to reach northern industrial towns like Blackburn, nevertheless created an environment where social mobility through talent and hard work became increasingly possible. This changing social landscape would ultimately enable McShane to pursue a career in acting, traditionally seen as a profession for the privileged classes.

Family Background and Influences

Ian McShane's family background played a crucial role in shaping his character and future career. His father, Harry McShane, was a professional footballer who played as a winger for Manchester United. This connection to the world of professional sports introduced young Ian to the concepts of discipline, public performance, and the pursuit of excellence from an early age.

Harry McShane's career with Manchester United spanned from 1938 to 1948, interrupted by World War II. His experiences as a professional athlete during this tumultuous period in British history provided a unique perspective that he likely shared with his son. The dedication required to maintain a sports career during wartime and the immediate post-war years demonstrated resilience and adaptability, traits that would later become hallmarks of Ian's acting career.

McShane's mother, Irene, played an equally important role in his upbringing. While less is publicly known about her, the influence of a strong maternal figure in a working-class Lancashire household of the 1940s and 1950s cannot be underestimated. The values of hard work, perseverance, and the importance of family were likely instilled in young Ian through his mother's guidance.

The McShane household, like many in post-war Britain, likely faced economic challenges. The experiences of managing a household during rationing and the gradual recovery of the 1950s would have taught young Ian valuable lessons about resourcefulness and adaptability. These early experiences may have contributed to his later ability to fully inhabit characters from various social backgrounds.

Growing up in a family with a father in the public eye exposed McShane to the realities of fame from an early age. He witnessed firsthand the adulation his father received as a Manchester United player, as well as the pressures and scrutiny that came with such a position. This early exposure to public life may have prepared him for his own future in the spotlight.

The influence of extended family and the close-knit community typical of northern industrial towns in the mid-20th century likely played a significant role in McShane's upbringing. Grandparents, aunts, uncles, and cousins often lived in close proximity, creating a support network and exposing young Ian to a variety of personalities and life experiences that would later inform his character portrayals.

Education was highly valued in many working-class families of the era, seen as a path to social mobility. McShane's parents likely encouraged his academic pursuits, leading to his attendance at Stretford Grammar School. This emphasis on education, combined with his father's career in sports, created an environment that valued both intellectual and physical achievements.

The cultural influences in the McShane household would have been a mix of traditional Lancashire working-class culture and the broader British popular culture of the post-war era. This might have included a love for variety shows, early television programs, and British cinema, all of which could have sparked

CHAPTER 1

McShane's interest in performance and storytelling.

Religion may have played a role in the McShane family's life, as it did for many British families of the era. The influence of religious teachings and the moral framework they provided could have contributed to McShane's understanding of human nature and moral complexity, elements he would later explore in many of his roles.

The McShane family's experiences during World War II, even though Ian was born towards its end, would have been a significant influence. Stories of wartime experiences, the challenges faced by the family and the community, and the sense of national unity during this period would have formed part of the family's narrative, shaping young Ian's worldview.

Growing Up in Post-War Britain

Ian McShane's formative years in post-war Britain were marked by a nation in transition. The Britain of the late 1940s and 1950s was a country rebuilding itself after the devastation of World War II. This period of reconstruction and social change provided the backdrop for McShane's childhood and adolescence, shaping his worldview and future career.

The immediate post-war years were characterized by austerity and rationing. Food, clothing, and fuel were scarce, and families like the McShanes had to make do with limited resources. This experience of scarcity likely instilled in young Ian a sense of resourcefulness and appreciation for simple pleasures, traits that would serve him well in his future career.

Education played a crucial role in McShane's upbringing. The implementation of the 1944 Education Act during his childhood years brought significant changes to the British education system. This act introduced the tripartite system of secondary education, consisting of grammar schools, secondary modern schools, and technical schools. McShane's attendance at Stretford Grammar School was a result of this new system, which aimed to provide opportunities based on aptitude rather than social class.

The 1950s saw the gradual emergence of youth culture in Britain. Teenagers, a concept that barely existed before the war, began to develop their own distinct identity. This emergence of youth culture, with its new music, fashion, and attitudes, would have been part of McShane's teenage experience, potentially influencing his later portrayals of rebellious or unconventional characters.

Television became increasingly common in British households during McShane's childhood. The coronation of Queen Elizabeth II in 1953, watched by millions on newly acquired television sets, marked a significant moment in British cultural life. This growing presence of television in everyday life may have sparked McShane's interest in the medium that would later become a significant part of his career.

The world of entertainment was undergoing significant changes during McShane's youth. British cinema was experiencing a renaissance, with films like "The Third Man" (1949) and "The Bridge on the River Kwai" (1957) achieving international acclaim. This golden age of British cinema may have influenced McShane's decision to pursue acting as a career.

Sports, particularly football, remained an important part of British cultural life in the post-war years. McShane's father's career as a professional footballer would have given young Ian a unique perspective on this aspect of British culture. The discipline and dedication required in professional sports may have influenced McShane's approach to his acting career.

The late 1950s and early 1960s saw the beginnings of significant social changes in Britain. The rigid class system began to show signs of weakening, and opportunities for social mobility increased. This changing social landscape made it possible for someone from McShane's background to

CHAPTER 1

consider a career in acting, traditionally seen as a profession for the upper classes.

The Cold War cast a long shadow over McShane's youth. The threat of nuclear conflict and the ideological battle between capitalism and communism were constant background concerns. This global tension may have contributed to the complexity and nuance McShane would later bring to his portrayals of characters caught in moral or political dilemmas.

Britain's relationship with its empire was changing dramatically during McShane's youth. The process of decolonization accelerated in the 1950s and 1960s, reshaping Britain's role on the world stage. This shifting global context would have been part of McShane's developing understanding of the world, potentially influencing his later ability to adapt to diverse roles and settings in his acting career.

CHAPTER 2

Education at Stretford Grammar School

Ian McShane's educational journey took a significant turn when he entered Stretford Grammar School. This institution, located in Stretford, Greater Manchester, played a crucial role in shaping McShane's academic and personal development during his formative years.

Stretford Grammar School, established in 1928, had already built a reputation for academic excellence by the time McShane attended in the 1950s. The school's ethos emphasized not only academic achievement but also the development of well-rounded individuals through extracurricular activities.

McShane's time at Stretford Grammar coincided with a period of significant changes in the British education system. The implementation of the 1944 Education Act had introduced the tripartite system, which divided secondary education into grammar schools, secondary modern schools, and technical schools. Grammar schools like Stretford were designed to provide an academically rigorous education to students who had passed the 11-plus examination.

CHAPTER 2

The curriculum at Stretford Grammar School was diverse and challenging. Students were exposed to a wide range of subjects, including English literature, mathematics, sciences, history, geography, and foreign languages. This broad educational base would later prove valuable to McShane in his acting career, providing him with a wealth of knowledge to draw upon in various roles.

English literature classes at Stretford Grammar likely played a particularly important role in nurturing McShane's interest in drama and performance. Exposure to classic works of British literature, including Shakespeare's plays, may have sparked his passion for acting and storytelling.

The school's emphasis on public speaking and debating provided McShane with early opportunities to develop his oratory skills. These experiences would have been invaluable in building his confidence and ability to express himself effectively, skills that would later become central to his acting career.

Extracurricular activities were an integral part of life at Stretford Grammar School. The school offered a range of clubs and societies, including a drama club. It was here that McShane likely had his first taste of formal acting, participating in school plays and performances.

Sports also played a significant role in the school's curriculum. Given McShane's family background in professional football, he may have excelled in athletic pursuits alongside his academic studies. This balance of physical and mental activities contributed to his overall development.

The teachers at Stretford Grammar School would have had a profound impact on McShane's educational journey. Dedicated educators who recognized and nurtured talent may have played a crucial role in encouraging McShane's early interest in acting and performance.

The social environment of Stretford Grammar School exposed McShane to a diverse group of peers from various backgrounds. This exposure to different perspectives and experiences would have broadened his worldview and enhanced his ability to understand and portray a wide range of characters in his future acting career.

McShane's academic performance at Stretford Grammar School set the stage for his future educational pursuits. His success in this academically rigorous environment demonstrated his intellectual capabilities and work ethic, traits that would serve him well in his later training as an actor.

The discipline instilled by the grammar school system, with its high expectations and structured approach to learning, likely contributed to McShane's ability to tackle the demands of a professional acting career. The habits of hard work and dedication formed during these years would prove invaluable in the competitive world of theater and film.

Royal Academy of Dramatic Art (RADA)

Ian McShane's journey into professional acting took a decisive turn with his acceptance into the Royal Academy of Dramatic Art (RADA). This prestigious institution, founded in 1904, has long been recognized as one of the world's leading drama schools, producing numerous renowned actors, directors, and theater professionals.

McShane's time at RADA began in 1960, marking the start of his formal training in the dramatic arts. The academy's rigorous program was designed to transform talented individuals into skilled, versatile actors capable of tackling a wide range of roles across various media.

The curriculum at RADA during McShane's time was comprehensive and demanding. Students were immersed in all aspects of acting, including voice training, movement, improvisation, textual analysis, and theater history. This holistic approach to actor training would provide McShane with a solid foundation for his future career.

Voice and speech training formed a crucial part of McShane's education at RADA. Students were taught to develop their vocal range, projection, and clarity, skills that would prove invaluable in both stage and screen performances. McShane's distinctive voice, which would later become one of his trademark features, was likely honed during this period.

Movement classes at RADA focused on developing physical awareness and expressiveness. Students learned various techniques to control and manipulate their bodies, enhancing their ability to physically embody different characters. These skills would later contribute to McShane's dynamic on-screen presence.

Textual analysis and interpretation were key components of the RADA curriculum. Students were taught to dissect and understand complex dramatic texts, from classical works to contemporary plays. This training would enable McShane to approach scripts with depth and insight throughout his career.

Practical performance experience was a central part of the RADA program. Students regularly participated in productions, allowing them to apply their learned skills in a practical setting. These performances, often attended by industry professionals, provided valuable exposure and experience.

The competitive nature of RADA pushed McShane to excel. The academy accepted only a small number of students each year, creating an environment of intense focus and dedication. This atmosphere of healthy competition would prepare McShane for the realities of the professional acting world.

Interaction with fellow students at RADA exposed McShane to a diverse range of talent and approaches to acting. Many of his classmates would go on to have successful careers in theater, film, and television, creating a network of professional connections that would prove valuable in his future career.

The faculty at RADA consisted of experienced actors, directors, and theater professionals who brought real-world expertise to their teaching. Their guidance and mentorship would have been instrumental in shaping McShane's approach to acting and his understanding of the industry.

RADA's location in London placed McShane at the heart of British theater. This proximity to the West End and other major theaters allowed students to immerse themselves in the vibrant London theater scene, attending performances and gaining inspiration from established actors.

The training at RADA emphasized versatility, preparing actors to work across different media including stage, film, television, and radio. This multi-faceted approach would later enable McShane to transition smoothly between these various forms throughout his career.

Graduation from RADA marked a significant milestone in McShane's journey as an actor. The skills, knowledge, and professional connections gained during his time at the academy would serve as a springboard for his entry into the professional acting world.

Early Theatre Experiences

Ian McShane's early theatre experiences laid the groundwork for his successful acting career. These formative performances, occurring in the years immediately following his graduation from RADA, provided crucial opportunities for McShane to apply his training and develop his craft in front of live audiences.

McShane's professional theatre debut came in 1962 with a production of

"The Promise" at the Arts Theatre in London. This play, written by Aleksei Arbuzov, was a challenging piece that required McShane to portray a complex character over several decades. The experience of sustaining a character through a full-length play in front of a discerning London audience was an invaluable learning experience for the young actor.

Following his debut, McShane quickly found more opportunities on the London stage. He appeared in productions at various theaters, including the Royal Court Theatre, known for its commitment to new writing and innovative productions. This exposure to contemporary plays helped McShane develop a versatility that would serve him well throughout his career.

One of McShane's significant early roles came in 1965 when he played Joe Orton in the premiere of John Hale's "Loot" at the Jeannetta Cochrane Theatre. This satirical black comedy pushed boundaries and caused controversy, providing McShane with experience in handling challenging and provocative material.

McShane's early theatre work was not confined to London. He also performed in regional theaters across the UK, gaining experience with different audiences and performance spaces. This touring work helped him build a reputation beyond the capital and exposed him to a wider range of theatrical traditions and styles.

Shakespeare featured prominently in McShane's early stage career. He took on roles in several of the Bard's plays, including performances with the Royal Shakespeare Company. These classical roles challenged McShane to master complex language and deeply nuanced characters, further honing his acting skills.

In addition to traditional theater, McShane also explored experimental and avant-garde productions during this period. These experiences pushed the boundaries of his training and encouraged him to take risks in his performances, contributing to his growth as a versatile actor.

McShane's early theatre work also included musical productions. While not primarily known as a musical theater performer, these experiences broadened his skill set and demonstrated his versatility as a performer. The discipline required in musical theater, combining acting, singing, and often dancing, further refined McShane's abilities as a well-rounded performer.

Critics began to take notice of McShane's performances during this period. Early reviews praised his intensity and ability to fully inhabit his characters. These positive responses helped build McShane's reputation within the industry and opened doors to more significant roles.

The community aspect of theater work was crucial in these early years. McShane formed professional relationships with directors, fellow actors, and other theater professionals that would prove valuable throughout his career. Many of these early connections led to future collaborations in theater, film, and television.

McShane's early theatre experiences also taught him the practical aspects of life as a working actor. The sometimes grueling schedule of rehearsals and performances, the need to maintain energy and focus night after night, and the importance of teamwork in theatrical productions all contributed to his professional development.

These formative years in theater instilled in McShane a deep respect for the craft of acting and the unique power of live performance. While his career would later expand significantly into film and television, the foundation laid during these early theatre experiences remained a core part of his approach to acting throughout his career.

3

CHAPTER 3

First TV Appearance: "Judas and the Black Messiah" (1962)

Ian McShane's television debut came in 1962 with an episode of the BBC series "Judas and the Black Messiah." This appearance marked the beginning of McShane's long and successful career in television.

The show, a religious drama, provided McShane with his first opportunity to showcase his acting skills to a television audience. His role, though small, was significant in launching his on-screen career. The experience of working in a television production was vastly different from his theatre work, requiring McShane to adapt his performance techniques to the intimacy of the camera.

"Judas and the Black Messiah" was part of a wave of religious programming popular on British television in the early 1960s. These productions often tackled complex moral and theological issues, providing young actors like McShane with meaty, challenging material to work with.

The technical aspects of television production in the early 1960s presented unique challenges. Most programs were broadcast live or recorded as-live, leaving little room for error. This high-pressure environment demanded quick thinking and adaptability from actors, skills that McShane would hone throughout his career.

McShane's performance in "Judas and the Black Messiah" caught the attention of television producers and casting directors. His ability to convey complex emotions in a subtle, camera-friendly manner set him apart from many of his peers who were more accustomed to the broader style of stage acting.

The experience of working on a television set exposed McShane to the collaborative nature of the medium. He interacted with directors, camera operators, sound technicians, and other crew members, gaining valuable insights into the production process that would serve him well in future roles.

This first television appearance also introduced McShane to the power of the medium to reach a wide audience. Unlike theatre, where performances were limited to those physically present, television allowed his work to be seen by viewers across the country. This broader exposure was crucial in building his reputation and fan base.

The period following his appearance in "Judas and the Black Messiah" saw McShane actively pursuing more television work. He began attending auditions specifically for TV roles, recognizing the growing importance of the medium in the entertainment industry.

McShane's performance in "Judas and the Black Messiah" also demonstrated his ability to handle period dramas and complex narratives. This versatility would become a hallmark of his career, allowing him to take on a wide range of roles across various genres.

The experience gained from this first television appearance helped McShane refine his approach to screen acting. He learned to modulate his performances, understanding that the camera could pick up nuances that might be lost on a theatre stage.

This early television role also exposed McShane to the fast-paced nature of TV production. Unlike theatre, where weeks of rehearsal preceded performances, television often required actors to prepare quickly and perform with minimal rehearsal time. This skill would prove invaluable throughout his career.

McShane's work on "Judas and the Black Messiah" also introduced him to the concept of typecasting in television. The role he played in this production could have easily led to him being offered similar parts in religious dramas. However, McShane's subsequent career choices demonstrate his determination to avoid being pigeonholed.

The critical reception of McShane's performance, though not widely documented due to the nature of the production, was positive enough to encourage him to pursue more television work. This early success laid the foundation for his future achievements in the medium.

"Lovejoy" and the Rise to Fame

Ian McShane's portrayal of the titular character in the BBC series "Lovejoy" marked a turning point in his career, catapulting him to widespread fame and establishing him as a household name in British television.

"Lovejoy," based on the novels by John Grant, premiered in 1986. The series followed the adventures of Lovejoy, a roguish antique dealer with an uncanny ability to spot genuine artifacts. McShane's charismatic performance brought the character to life, infusing him with a mix of charm, wit, and a hint of mischief that resonated with audiences.

The show's premise allowed McShane to showcase his versatility as an actor. Each episode presented new challenges as Lovejoy navigated the world of antiques, often finding himself embroiled in mysteries and schemes. McShane's ability to balance comedy and drama within the character was key to the show's success.

"Lovejoy" ran for six series between 1986 and 1994, totaling 71 episodes. This long run provided McShane with a level of job security and public exposure that was rare in the often unpredictable world of acting. It also allowed him to deeply explore and develop the character over time.

The show's popularity extended beyond the UK, with international broadcasts bringing McShane's performance to a global audience. This wider exposure significantly boosted his profile and opened doors to international opportunities later in his career.

McShane's involvement in "Lovejoy" went beyond his on-screen role. He became an executive producer for the later series, giving him a say in the show's direction and demonstrating his growing influence in the television industry.

The character of Lovejoy became so closely associated with McShane that it risked typecasting him. However, his nuanced performance and subsequent career choices proved his range extended far beyond this beloved character.

"Lovejoy" 's success also highlighted McShane's appeal as a leading man. His ability to carry a series demonstrated his star power and led to more prominent roles in both television and film.

The show's format, blending elements of comedy, drama, and mystery, allowed McShane to display a wide range of acting skills. This versatility would become a hallmark of his career, enabling him to tackle diverse roles in various genres.

"Lovejoy" 's impact on popular culture was significant. The show sparked interest in antiques among the general public and even influenced the antiques trade itself. McShane's portrayal became a cultural touchstone, often referenced in British media.

The series' long run provided McShane with valuable experience in the technical aspects of television production. Working on a single show for several years allowed him to refine his screen acting techniques and develop a deep understanding of the medium.

"Lovejoy" also showcased McShane's ability to build chemistry with his co-stars. His interactions with the show's ensemble cast were a key factor in its success, demonstrating his skill in collaborative performances.

The show's popularity led to increased media attention for McShane. He became a regular fixture in interviews and talk shows, honing his public persona and becoming comfortable with the fame that came with his success.

Notable Early TV Roles

Before and after his breakthrough in "Lovejoy," Ian McShane took on several notable television roles that showcased his versatility and contributed to his growing reputation as a skilled character actor.

In 1967, McShane appeared in an episode of "Wuthering Heights," a BBC adaptation of Emily Brontë's classic novel. His portrayal of Heathcliff demonstrated his ability to handle complex, brooding characters and period dramas. This role helped establish him as a serious dramatic actor capable of tackling literary adaptations.

McShane's performance in the 1971 BBC play "Villain" further cemented his reputation. In this gritty crime drama, he played a ruthless gangster, showcasing a darker side of his acting range. The role was a significant departure from his earlier work and proved his ability to portray morally ambiguous characters convincingly.

The 1975 series "Space: 1999" saw McShane venturing into science fiction. His guest appearance in this popular show demonstrated his adaptability across genres and his appeal to a wider, international audience. The experience of working on a high-concept series with extensive special effects also broadened his skill set as an actor.

In 1977, McShane took on the role of Judas Iscariot in the landmark miniseries "Jesus of Nazareth." This high-profile production, directed by Franco Zeffirelli, featured an all-star international cast. McShane's nuanced portrayal of one of history's most infamous figures showcased his ability to bring depth and humanity to controversial characters.

The 1980 series "Disraeli" saw McShane in the title role of the famous British Prime Minister. This biographical drama allowed him to demonstrate his skill with historical figures and political narratives. The role required extensive research and a subtle approach to portraying a well-known public figure, further expanding McShane's acting repertoire.

McShane's appearance in the 1982 TV movie "The Letter" opposite Lee Remick was another significant early role. Based on the play by W. Somerset Maugham, this production allowed McShane to work alongside established Hollywood talent, further raising his profile in the industry.

In 1985, McShane starred in "Evergreen," a miniseries based on Belva Plain's novel. This sweeping historical drama spanned several decades and required McShane to portray his character at different stages of life. The role demonstrated his ability to carry a long-form narrative and maintain character consistency over an extended storyline.

Throughout the 1980s, McShane made guest appearances on popular British

CHAPTER 3

television shows such as "Magnum, P.I." and "Miami Vice." These roles, while brief, kept him in the public eye and showcased his ability to make an impact in short screen times.

The 1988 TV movie "War and Remembrance" saw McShane in a supporting role in this epic World War II drama. The production's scale and international cast provided valuable experience in working on large, complex television projects.

McShane's role in the 1989 series "Dallas" marked his entry into American primetime soap operas. Playing a English cousin of the Ewing family, McShane brought his characteristic charm and depth to the long-running series, further expanding his visibility to American audiences.

These early television roles collectively demonstrate McShane's range as an actor, his ability to adapt to different genres and production styles, and his steady rise in the television industry. Each role contributed to his growing reputation, setting the stage for his later success in both television and film.

CHAPTER 4

Film Debut: "The Wild and the Willing" (1962)

Ian McShane's transition from stage to screen began with his film debut in "The Wild and the Willing" (1962). This British drama, directed by Ralph Thomas, marked McShane's first appearance on the silver screen and set the stage for his future in cinema.

"The Wild and the Willing" focused on the lives of university students in the early 1960s. McShane played Harry Brown, a working-class student struggling to fit in with his more privileged peers. The role allowed McShane to draw on his own background and experiences, bringing authenticity to his performance.

The film's themes of class struggle and social mobility resonated with British audiences of the time. McShane's portrayal of Harry Brown captured the frustrations and ambitions of a generation seeking to break free from traditional class boundaries.

Working on a film set presented new challenges for McShane. The technical aspects of filmmaking, such as hitting marks and maintaining continuity between takes, required a different skill set from his stage work. McShane quickly adapted to these demands, demonstrating his versatility as an actor.

"The Wild and the Willing" also introduced McShane to the collaborative nature of filmmaking. He worked closely with director Ralph Thomas and his co-stars, including John Hurt and Samantha Eggar, both of whom would go on to have successful careers in film.

The experience of seeing himself on the big screen for the first time was a pivotal moment in McShane's career. It solidified his desire to pursue film acting alongside his stage and television work.

Critical reception of "The Wild and the Willing" was mixed, but McShane's performance was generally well-received. Critics noted his natural screen presence and ability to convey complex emotions with subtlety.

The film's release coincided with the British New Wave cinema movement, which focused on realistic depictions of working-class life. While not strictly part of this movement, "The Wild and the Willing" shared some of its themes and aesthetic sensibilities.

McShane's performance in the film caught the attention of other filmmakers and casting directors. It opened doors for future film roles and helped establish him as a versatile young actor capable of tackling both stage and screen work.

The experience of promoting "The Wild and the Willing" introduced McShane to another aspect of the film industry. He participated in interviews and press events, developing skills in public relations that would serve him well throughout his career.

Working on "The Wild and the Willing" also exposed McShane to the business side of filmmaking. He began to understand the importance of box office performance and the role of marketing in a film's success.

The film's exploration of youth culture and changing social norms in 1960s Britain provided McShane with material that was both culturally relevant and dramatically rich. This experience likely influenced his future choice of roles, as he continued to seek out projects that engaged with contemporary issues.

"The Wild and the Willing" also marked McShane's first experience with the permanence of film performances. Unlike stage work, where each performance is unique, his work in this film would be viewed and reviewed for years to come, adding a new dimension to his understanding of his craft.

Breakthrough Role: "If It's Tuesday, This Must Be Belgium" (1969)

Seven years after his film debut, Ian McShane landed a role that would significantly boost his profile in the film industry. "If It's Tuesday, This Must Be Belgium" (1969) provided McShane with a platform to showcase his talents to a wider, international audience.

The film, a romantic comedy directed by Mel Stuart, followed the misadventures of American tourists on a whirlwind tour of Europe. McShane played Charlie Cartwright, a charming tour guide who becomes romantically involved with one of the tourists.

McShane's portrayal of Charlie Cartwright allowed him to display his comedic timing and charm. The role was a departure from his earlier, more dramatic work, demonstrating his versatility as an actor and his ability to adapt to different genres.

CHAPTER 4

"If It's Tuesday, This Must Be Belgium" was a commercial success, particularly in the United States. The film's popularity exposed McShane to American audiences and Hollywood producers, opening up new opportunities for his career.

The international nature of the production provided McShane with valuable experience working on a larger scale film. Shot on location across Europe, the film introduced him to the challenges and rewards of working in different countries and cultures.

McShane's performance in the film received positive reviews from critics. Many noted his charisma and screen presence, predicting a bright future for the young actor in Hollywood productions.

Working alongside established stars like Suzanne Pleshette and Norman Fell gave McShane the opportunity to learn from experienced film actors. This exposure to different acting styles and techniques further refined his approach to screen acting.

The success of "If It's Tuesday, This Must Be Belgium" led to more film offers for McShane. It marked a turning point in his career, shifting his focus more towards film work alongside his ongoing television and stage commitments.

The film's light-hearted tone and broad appeal demonstrated McShane's ability to connect with mainstream audiences. This commercial success would prove crucial in securing future roles and establishing him as a bankable film actor.

McShane's character in the film, Charlie Cartwright, became something of a fan favorite. The role showcased McShane's ability to create memorable, likable characters, a skill that would serve him well throughout his career.

The experience of promoting "If It's Tuesday, This Must Be Belgium" on an international scale was new for McShane. He participated in press tours and interviews across multiple countries, further raising his global profile.

The film's success also introduced McShane to the potential financial rewards of a hit movie. This new aspect of his career likely influenced his future decisions about balancing film work with his other acting commitments.

McShane's performance in "If It's Tuesday, This Must Be Belgium" caught the attention of casting directors and producers on both sides of the Atlantic. It opened doors to a wider range of roles and began to establish him as a transatlantic talent.

The film's blend of comedy and romance allowed McShane to demonstrate his range as an actor. His ability to handle both humorous and emotional scenes with equal skill set him apart from many of his contemporaries.

Balancing Film and Television Work

Following his breakthrough in "If It's Tuesday, This Must Be Belgium," Ian McShane faced the challenge of balancing his burgeoning film career with his established television work. This period of his career was marked by a diverse range of projects across both mediums.

McShane's approach to this balancing act was pragmatic. He recognized the different strengths and opportunities offered by film and television, and sought to leverage both to further his career. This strategy allowed him to maintain a steady presence on screen while pursuing more challenging or prestigious roles in film.

In the 1970s, McShane continued to take on television roles while building his film career. He appeared in several British television series and made-for-TV movies, including "Wuthering Heights" (1967) and "The Last of the

Mohicans" (1971). These projects kept him in the public eye and provided a steady income between film roles.

On the film front, McShane appeared in a variety of productions throughout the 1970s and 1980s. Notable films from this period include "Villain" (1971), where he played a violent gangster, and "Yesterday's Hero" (1979), a sports drama. These roles allowed him to explore different genres and characters, expanding his range as an actor.

McShane's ability to move between film and television was aided by the changing nature of the entertainment industry. The line between the two mediums was becoming increasingly blurred, with many actors freely transitioning between them without the stigma that had previously been attached to television work.

The different pacing of film and television production presented both challenges and opportunities for McShane. Television work often required a faster turnaround, with less rehearsal time and more pages of dialogue to learn each day. Film, on the other hand, often allowed for more detailed character development and scene preparation.

McShane's experience in both mediums made him a versatile and sought-after actor. He could adapt to the demands of a film set or a television studio with equal ease, making him an attractive option for producers in both industries.

The financial aspects of balancing film and television work also played a role in McShane's career decisions. While film roles often came with higher prestige, television work could provide more consistent income. McShane navigated these considerations skillfully, building a stable career while still pursuing challenging and rewarding roles.

McShane's work in both film and television allowed him to build a diverse fan base. Television roles kept him in regular contact with audiences, while film appearances allowed him to reach new viewers and tackle more varied characters.

The skills McShane developed in each medium often complemented his work in the other. The intimacy and immediacy required for television performances enhanced his film work, while the larger-than-life aspects of some film roles brought new energy to his television performances.

McShane's ability to balance film and television work also allowed him to weather the ups and downs of the entertainment industry. When opportunities in one medium were scarce, he could often find work in the other, maintaining career momentum.

The variety of roles offered by working in both film and television kept McShane's career fresh and challenging. He avoided typecasting by constantly switching between different types of characters and genres across both mediums.

McShane's success in balancing film and television work set a template for many actors who followed. His career demonstrated that it was possible to maintain a presence in both mediums without sacrificing quality or opportunities.

The experience gained from working in both film and television contributed to McShane's growth as an actor. He developed a nuanced understanding of the technical and artistic differences between the two mediums, enhancing his performances in both.

5

CHAPTER 5

Creating the Iconic Character

Ian McShane's portrayal of Lovejoy, the roguish antique dealer with a heart of gold, became a defining role in his career. The character, originally created by John Grant in a series of novels, took on new life when McShane brought him to the small screen.

Lovejoy's character was a unique blend of charm, wit, and moral ambiguity. McShane worked closely with the show's writers to develop a nuanced portrayal that would resonate with audiences. He infused Lovejoy with a rakish charm and a twinkle in his eye that made the character instantly likable, even when engaged in less-than-legal activities.

The physical appearance of Lovejoy was carefully crafted to match the character's personality. McShane adopted a distinctive look for the role, including long hair and a wardrobe that blended contemporary style with vintage pieces. This visual representation became integral to the character's appeal and instantly recognizable to viewers.

Lovejoy's expertise in antiques was a crucial aspect of the character. McShane immersed himself in the world of antiques, learning about various periods and styles to lend authenticity to his performance. This dedication to the craft allowed him to deliver lines about obscure antiques and their history with conviction and ease.

The character's moral compass was a key element that McShane had to navigate. Lovejoy often skirted the edges of legality in his dealings, but always maintained a personal code of ethics. McShane's portrayal balanced these aspects skillfully, making Lovejoy a complex and intriguing protagonist.

Lovejoy's relationships with other characters in the show were crucial to defining his personality. McShane developed a strong on-screen rapport with his co-stars, particularly Phyllis Logan as Lady Jane and Chris Jury as Eric. These relationships added depth to Lovejoy's character and provided opportunities for both dramatic and comedic moments.

The character's fourth-wall-breaking asides to the camera were a unique feature that McShane had to master. These direct addresses to the audience required a delicate touch to avoid coming across as gimmicky. McShane's delivery of these moments became a hallmark of the show, drawing viewers into Lovejoy's world and thought processes.

Lovejoy's charm with women was a significant aspect of the character. McShane portrayed this facet of Lovejoy with a light touch, making the character appealing without becoming a caricature. This element of Lovejoy's personality added a romantic subplot to many episodes and contributed to the show's broad appeal.

The character's knowledge of antiques and his ability to spot a fake or find hidden treasures was central to many plotlines. McShane had to convey this expertise convincingly, often explaining complex concepts about antiques to both characters in the show and the audience at home. His delivery of these explanations became an art form in itself, educating viewers while advancing the plot.

Lovejoy's sense of humor was a key component of his charm. McShane infused the character with a dry wit and a penchant for clever wordplay. This humor often served to defuse tense situations in the show and became a beloved aspect of Lovejoy's personality.

The evolution of Lovejoy's character over the course of the series was subtle but significant. McShane worked with the writers to allow Lovejoy to grow and change, while maintaining the core elements that made him popular. This evolution kept the character fresh and engaging throughout the show's six-season run.

McShane's portrayal of Lovejoy was so convincing that many viewers began to associate him closely with the character. This level of identification with a role can be both a blessing and a curse for an actor, and McShane had to navigate the fine line between embracing the popularity of Lovejoy and avoiding being typecast.

Impact on British Television

"Lovejoy" made a significant impact on British television during its run from 1986 to 1994. The show's unique blend of drama, comedy, and mystery set it apart from other programming of the time and helped to redefine what a British television series could be.

The show's success demonstrated the appetite for character-driven series that didn't fit neatly into established genres. "Lovejoy" combined elements of crime drama, romantic comedy, and even educational content about antiques, creating a formula that proved highly popular with viewers.

"Lovejoy" played a role in revitalizing Sunday night television in the UK. Its primetime slot on BBC1 attracted a large and loyal audience, establishing Sunday evening as a key time for quality drama on British television. This scheduling strategy influenced future programming decisions across British networks.

The series' focus on the world of antiques had a noticeable effect on public interest in the subject. Many viewers were inspired to learn more about antiques and collectibles, leading to increased attendance at antique fairs and a general uptick in the antiques trade. This phenomenon, sometimes referred to as the "Lovejoy effect," demonstrated the power of television to influence public interests and trends.

"Lovejoy" also showcased the beauty of the English countryside, particularly East Anglia where much of the series was filmed. This exposure boosted tourism in the region and inspired other productions to venture outside of urban settings, highlighting the diverse landscapes of Britain.

The show's format, with its self-contained episodes featuring a mystery or scheme centered around antiques, provided a template for future series. It demonstrated how a niche interest like antique dealing could be used as a framework for compelling storytelling.

"Lovejoy" 's success paved the way for other quirky, character-driven series on British television. It showed that audiences were receptive to shows that didn't fit the mold of traditional police procedurals or sitcoms, encouraging producers and networks to take more risks with unconventional concepts.

The series also had an impact on the portrayal of class on British television. Lovejoy, with his working-class background and connections to the world of aristocracy through characters like Lady Jane, provided a nuanced exploration of class dynamics in contemporary Britain.

CHAPTER 5

"Lovejoy" 's international success, particularly in the United States, helped to raise the profile of British television abroad. It demonstrated that British series could appeal to a global audience, paving the way for future international hits.

The show's long run and consistent quality set a high standard for British television production. It showed that a series could maintain its appeal over many seasons without sacrificing quality or resorting to gimmicks.

"Lovejoy" also had an impact on the careers of its cast and crew. Many of the actors, writers, and directors who worked on the show went on to have successful careers in British television and film, their experiences on "Lovejoy" serving as a valuable stepping stone.

The series' handling of its leading man, allowing Ian McShane to shape and develop the character of Lovejoy, influenced how other shows approached their protagonists. It demonstrated the benefits of giving talented actors the freedom to contribute to character development.

Behind the Scenes of "Lovejoy"

The production of "Lovejoy" was a complex operation that involved a dedicated team of professionals both in front of and behind the camera. The show's success was the result of their collective efforts and creativity.

Filming locations played a crucial role in creating the atmosphere of "Lovejoy." The production team scouted numerous locations across East Anglia to find the perfect settings for each episode. This attention to detail in location selection contributed significantly to the show's authentic feel and visual appeal.

The costume department faced the challenge of dressing characters in a way that was both contemporary and timeless. Lovejoy's distinctive look, with his long hair and eclectic wardrobe, was carefully crafted to reflect his character. The team also had to source and create period-appropriate costumes for flashback scenes and when dealing with antiques from different eras.

Props were a crucial element of "Lovejoy," given the show's focus on antiques. The props department worked tirelessly to source genuine antiques or create convincing replicas for use in the show. This attention to detail was essential for maintaining the credibility of Lovejoy's expertise.

The writing process for "Lovejoy" was collaborative and ongoing. While the show was based on John Grant's novels, the television scripts often deviated from the source material to create stories better suited for the screen. Writers worked closely with the cast, particularly Ian McShane, to develop plots and dialogue that played to the actors' strengths.

Director of Photography: The visual style of "Lovejoy" was carefully crafted to enhance the show's themes and settings. The cinematography had to capture both the beauty of the East Anglian countryside and the intricate details of the antiques featured in each episode. This required a skilled and adaptable approach to lighting and camera work.

The editing process for "Lovejoy" was crucial in maintaining the show's pace and tone. Editors had to balance the mystery elements of each episode with character development and comedic moments, ensuring that each episode flowed smoothly and kept viewers engaged.

Music played a significant role in setting the tone of "Lovejoy." The show's composer created a distinctive theme and incidental music that complemented the on-screen action without overpowering it. The music often had to evoke different historical periods to match the antiques featured in each episode.

CHAPTER 5

The production schedule for "Lovejoy" was demanding, with multiple episodes being filmed simultaneously to meet broadcast deadlines. This required careful planning and coordination to ensure that cast and crew were where they needed to be and that all necessary resources were available.

Research was an ongoing process throughout the production of "Lovejoy." The show's commitment to accuracy in its portrayal of the antiques world meant that experts were often consulted to verify details about specific items or historical periods.

The special effects team, while not as prominent as in some other productions, played an important role in "Lovejoy." They were responsible for creating convincing reproductions of valuable antiques that could be safely handled on set, as well as any necessary visual effects for the show's occasional forays into historical flashbacks.

The production of "Lovejoy" also involved a significant logistical operation. Coordinating the movement of cast, crew, and equipment around various locations in East Anglia required careful planning and execution.

The show's producers played a crucial role in managing the overall vision of "Lovejoy." They had to balance creative decisions with practical and financial considerations, ensuring that the show maintained its quality and appeal while staying within budget.

6

CHAPTER 6

Hollywood Calling

Breaking into American Cinema

Ian McShane's journey to Hollywood began with a determination to expand his acting horizons beyond British television and film. The allure of American cinema beckoned, promising new challenges and opportunities for the versatile actor.

McShane's initial foray into Hollywood productions came through supporting roles in films that showcased his ability to adapt to different genres and characters. His distinctive voice and commanding presence quickly caught the attention of American directors and producers.

One of McShane's early breaks in Hollywood came with his role in the 1985 miniseries "A.D." This biblical epic, produced for American television, allowed McShane to demonstrate his range to a wider audience and establish connections within the U.S. entertainment industry.

The transition to American cinema wasn't without its challenges. McShane had to navigate a different industry culture, adapt to new filming techniques, and compete with established Hollywood actors for roles. His persistence and talent eventually paid off, leading to more substantial parts in American productions.

McShane's breakthrough in Hollywood came with his role in the 2000 film "Sexy Beast." His portrayal of Teddy Bass, a menacing gangster, garnered critical acclaim and put him firmly on the radar of Hollywood casting directors. This performance showcased McShane's ability to bring depth and complexity to villainous characters.

Following "Sexy Beast," McShane began to receive offers for more prominent roles in American films. His ability to seamlessly switch between British and American accents made him a versatile choice for a variety of characters, further expanding his opportunities in Hollywood.

McShane's success in breaking into American cinema served as an inspiration for other British actors looking to make the leap across the pond. His journey demonstrated that with persistence, talent, and the right opportunities, it was possible to build a successful career in both British and American entertainment industries.

Notable Film Roles in the 1990s and 2000s

The 1990s and 2000s marked a prolific period in Ian McShane's film career, with a string of memorable roles that showcased his versatility and screen presence.

In 1994, McShane appeared in "Princess Caraboo," a period drama where he played the role of Frixos. This film allowed him to display his talent for historical characters and period pieces, a skill that would serve him well throughout his career.

McShane's role in the 2003 film "Agent Cody Banks" introduced him to a younger audience. Playing the villainous Dr. Brinkman, McShane demonstrated his ability to adapt his acting style to family-friendly entertainment while still maintaining his trademark intensity.

2005 saw McShane take on the role of Merriman Lyon in "The Dark Is Rising," a fantasy adventure film based on the novel by Susan Cooper. This role allowed McShane to explore the fantasy genre and work with special effects, further expanding his repertoire.

McShane's portrayal of Captain Hook in the 2003 film "Peter Pan" was particularly noteworthy. His interpretation of the classic villain brought a new depth to the character, blending menace with a touch of humor and pathos.

In 2006, McShane voiced the character of Captain Victor Maynard in the animated film "Shrek the Third." This role showcased McShane's voice acting skills and his ability to bring characters to life without relying on his physical presence on screen.

McShane's role in the 2007 film "Hot Rod" demonstrated his comedic timing. Playing the stepfather to Andy Samberg's character, McShane proved that he could hold his own in a comedy alongside established comedic actors.

The 2008 film "Death Race" saw McShane in the role of Coach, a gritty and hardened character in a dystopian action film. This performance highlighted McShane's ability to bring gravitas to even the most outlandish and high-octane scenarios.

CHAPTER 6

Working with Hollywood's Elite

Throughout his career in Hollywood, Ian McShane had the opportunity to work alongside some of the industry's most respected and talented individuals, both in front of and behind the camera.

McShane's role in the 2003 film "Nemesis Game" brought him into contact with director Jesse Warn and actors Adrian Paul and Carly Pope. This thriller allowed McShane to work in an ensemble cast, showcasing his ability to build complex on-screen relationships.

In the 2007 film "The Seeker: The Dark Is Rising," McShane worked with director David L. Cunningham and shared screen time with young actors Alexander Ludwig and Christopher Eccleston. This experience allowed McShane to mentor younger actors while also collaborating with seasoned professionals.

McShane's involvement in the 2008 film "Death Race" put him on set with action star Jason Statham and director Paul W.S. Anderson. This high-octane production gave McShane the chance to work within the fast-paced world of action filmmaking and collaborate with experts in the genre.

The 2010 remake of "The Pillars of the Earth" miniseries saw McShane working with an international cast including Matthew Macfadyen, Eddie Redmayne, and Hayley Atwell. This project allowed McShane to return to his roots in historical drama while working with a new generation of British and American actors.

In 2011, McShane joined the cast of "Pirates of the Caribbean: On Stranger Tides," working alongside Hollywood heavyweights Johnny Depp and Penélope Cruz. This blockbuster production exposed McShane to the world of big-budget filmmaking and special effects.

McShane's role in the 2014 film "Hercules" brought him into collaboration with Dwayne "The Rock" Johnson and director Brett Ratner. This project allowed McShane to work in the realm of mythological epic films, adding another genre to his diverse filmography.

Throughout these collaborations, McShane's professionalism and dedication to his craft earned him the respect of his co-stars and directors. His ability to adapt to different working styles and bring depth to his characters made him a valuable asset on any production.

McShane's experiences working with Hollywood's elite not only enhanced his own skills as an actor but also allowed him to contribute his expertise to each project. His collaborative spirit and willingness to learn from others, regardless of their age or experience level, made him a beloved figure on set.

7

CHAPTER 7

Reinvention with "Black Hills' Antihero"

Portraying Al Swearengen

Ian McShane's portrayal of Al Swearengen in HBO's "Black Hills' Antihero" marked a pivotal moment in his career. The role demanded a level of complexity and nuance that McShane embraced with gusto.

Swearengen, the proprietor of the Gem Saloon, embodied the gritty essence of the American frontier. McShane infused the character with a potent mix of ruthlessness and charm, creating a captivating antihero that viewers couldn't help but be drawn to.

The actor's preparation for the role was meticulous. He delved into historical accounts of the real Black Hills' Antihero, studying the mannerisms and speech patterns of the era. This dedication to authenticity shone through in his performance, bringing a lived-in quality to Swearengen that made him feel like a product of his harsh environment.

McShane's delivery of Swearengen's profanity-laden dialogue became legendary. He turned the character's colorful language into a form of poetry, each curse and insult delivered with precision and intent. This linguistic mastery added depth to Swearengen, revealing the intelligence behind his brutish exterior.

The physical transformation McShane underwent for the role was striking. He adopted Swearengen's distinctive facial hair and period-appropriate attire, disappearing into the character so completely that viewers often forgot they were watching Ian McShane.

McShane's portrayal highlighted Swearengen's strategic mind. He showed how the character manipulated those around him, always three steps ahead in the town's power struggles. This chess master approach to the role added layers of intrigue to every scene Swearengen appeared in.

The actor brought a surprising vulnerability to Swearengen. In quiet moments, McShane revealed the character's hidden depths, hinting at past traumas and inner conflicts that drove his actions. This multifaceted approach made Swearengen a character that defied simple categorization.

McShane's chemistry with his co-stars elevated every scene. His interactions with Timothy Olyphant's Seth Bullock crackled with tension, while his scenes with Paula Malcomson's Trixie revealed unexpected tenderness. These relationships showcased McShane's ability to adapt his performance to different dynamics.

The role required McShane to navigate complex moral territory. Swearengen committed heinous acts, yet McShane found ways to make the character, if not sympathetic, at least understandable. This balancing act kept viewers engaged, never sure whether to root for or against Swearengen.

McShane's commitment to the role extended beyond his on-screen performance. He immersed himself in the world of "Black Hills' Antihero," contributing ideas to the writers and collaborating closely with the show's creator, David Milch, to develop Swearengen's arc over the series.

The physical demands of the role were considerable. McShane threw himself into Swearengen's violent confrontations, bringing a raw energy to the character's fights and brawls. This physicality added another dimension to his portrayal, emphasizing Swearengen's dangerous nature.

Through his portrayal of Al Swearengen, McShane created an iconic television character. His performance set a new standard for antiheroes on the small screen, influencing countless shows that followed. The role of Swearengen will forever be associated with McShane, a testament to the indelible impression he made in "Black Hills' Antihero."

Critical Acclaim and Awards

The critical response to Ian McShane's portrayal of Al Swearengen in "Black Hills' Antihero" was overwhelmingly positive. Critics praised his ability to make such a morally ambiguous character compelling and even, at times, sympathetic.

McShane's performance earned him a Golden Globe Award for Best Actor in a Television Series Drama in 2005. This recognition from his peers in the industry solidified his status as one of television's top actors.

The actor also received a Primetime Emmy Award nomination for Outstanding Lead Actor in a Drama Series in 2005. While he didn't win, the nomination itself was a testament to the impact of his performance.

Critics particularly lauded McShane's delivery of the show's profanity-laced dialogue. Many noted how he elevated the crude language to an art form, finding musicality and depth in Swearengen's colorful vocabulary.

The Television Critics Association recognized McShane's work with a nomination for Individual Achievement in Drama in 2004. This nod from television critics further underscored the widespread appreciation for his portrayal of Swearengen.

McShane's performance was often singled out in reviews of "Black Hills' Antihero." Critics frequently cited his scenes as highlights of the series, praising his ability to command the screen and elevate the material.

The actor's work on "Black Hills' Antihero" earned him a place on numerous "Best TV Performances" lists. These accolades came not just from entertainment publications, but from respected mainstream news outlets as well.

McShane's portrayal of Swearengen was often compared favorably to other iconic television antiheroes. Critics placed him in the same league as James Gandolfini's Tony Soprano and Bryan Cranston's Walter White.

The Screen Actors Guild also recognized McShane's work, nominating him for Outstanding Performance by a Male Actor in a Drama Series in 2005. This acknowledgment from his fellow actors highlighted the respect he had earned within the industry.

Critics praised McShane's ability to convey complex emotions with minimal dialogue. His expressive face and subtle body language were often cited as key elements of his powerful performance.

McShane's work on "Black Hills' Antihero" was not just acclaimed in the United States. International critics also praised his performance, helping to raise his profile globally.

The critical consensus was that McShane had created one of television's most memorable characters. His portrayal of Swearengen was seen as a masterclass in acting, setting a new benchmark for television performances.

Impact on McShane's Career

Ian McShane's role as Al Swearengen in "Black Hills' Antihero" significantly altered the trajectory of his career. The critically acclaimed performance opened up new opportunities and changed how he was perceived in the industry.

Post-"Black Hills' Antihero," McShane found himself in high demand for complex, morally ambiguous roles. Casting directors and filmmakers sought him out for characters that required the depth and nuance he had displayed as Swearengen.

The success of "Black Hills' Antihero" elevated McShane's status in Hollywood. He transitioned from being primarily known for his work in British television to becoming a respected figure in American prestige TV and film.

McShane's performance as Swearengen showcased his ability to carry a series. This led to more leading roles in television, including the short-lived but critically acclaimed series "Kings."

The actor's work on "Black Hills' Antihero" also impacted the types of film roles he was offered. He began to receive more substantial parts in major Hollywood productions, moving beyond the supporting character actor roles he had often played before.

McShane's newfound reputation as a captivating antihero led to his casting in the "John Wick" franchise. His portrayal of Winston, the enigmatic owner of the Continental Hotel, drew parallels to his work as Swearengen.

The critical acclaim for his "Black Hills' Antihero" performance gave McShane more leverage in choosing his roles. He could be more selective, gravitating towards projects that offered complex, challenging characters.

McShane's work on the show also opened doors in the world of voice acting. His distinctive voice, which had been such a crucial part of Swearengen's character, became highly sought after for animated films and video games.

The actor's experience on "Black Hills' Antihero" influenced his approach to subsequent roles. He brought the same level of intensity and preparation to his post-"Black Hills' Antihero" work, raising the bar for his own performances.

McShane's success with "Black Hills' Antihero" allowed him to take more risks in his career. He felt empowered to tackle unconventional roles and projects that he might not have considered before.

The show's impact extended beyond acting opportunities. McShane found himself in demand for interviews and panel discussions, where he could share insights about his craft and the television industry.

"Black Hills' Antihero" cemented McShane's legacy in television history. His portrayal of Swearengen will likely be remembered as one of his defining roles, influencing how future generations of actors and audiences perceive him.

8

CHAPTER 8

Voice Acting and Animation

Exploring New Mediums

Ian McShane's venture into voice acting opened up a new dimension in his career. This shift allowed him to explore characters and stories beyond the constraints of physical appearance or age.

McShane's distinctive voice, with its rich timbre and expressive range, proved to be a valuable asset in the world of animation and voice-over work. His ability to convey complex emotions through vocal performance alone made him a sought-after talent in this field.

The transition to voice acting required McShane to adapt his acting techniques. Without the ability to rely on facial expressions or body language, he had to channel all of his character's personality and emotions through his voice alone.

Voice acting offered McShane the opportunity to take on roles that would have been impossible in live-action. He could portray characters of any age, species, or fantastical nature, expanding his range as an actor.

McShane embraced the technical challenges of voice acting. He learned to work with sound engineers and directors in a recording booth, mastering the art of timing his performance to match animated visuals or pre-existing footage.

The world of animation allowed McShane to participate in projects with broader appeal, including family-friendly films and television shows. This expanded his audience beyond the adult-oriented dramas he was typically associated with.

Voice acting also provided McShane with a new level of creative freedom. He could experiment with different vocal techniques and characterizations without the limitations of physical performance.

McShane's foray into voice acting coincided with a boom in the animation industry. The increasing quality and popularity of animated films and TV shows meant that his voice work reached large, diverse audiences.

The actor found that voice acting allowed him to take on multiple roles in a single project. In some animated productions, he voiced several characters, showcasing his versatility as a performer.

Voice acting also offered McShane a different pace of work. Recording sessions for animated projects often allowed for a more flexible schedule than live-action filming, giving him the opportunity to balance multiple projects simultaneously.

McShane's success in voice acting influenced other aspects of his career. His improved vocal control and expressiveness enhanced his live-action performances, particularly in roles that required voiceover narration.

The skills McShane developed through voice acting also proved useful in his stage work. His enhanced vocal projection and control allowed him to command larger theatrical spaces with ease.

Notable Voice Roles

Ian McShane's voice acting career includes a diverse range of memorable characters across various mediums. His work in animation showcases his versatility and ability to bring depth to even the most fantastical roles.

In the animated film "Coraline" (2009), McShane voiced Mr. Bobinsky, an eccentric Russian acrobat. His performance captured the character's mysterious and slightly sinister nature, adding depth to the film's eerie atmosphere.

McShane lent his voice to the character of Tai Lung in "Kung Fu Panda" (2008). His portrayal of the vengeful snow leopard villain demonstrated his ability to convey menace and power through voice alone.

The actor took on the role of Captain Hook in the animated series "Jake and the Never Land Pirates" (2011-2016). This family-friendly interpretation of the classic villain allowed McShane to explore a more comedic side of voice acting.

In "The Golden Compass" (2007), McShane voiced Ragnar Sturlusson, the king of the armored bears. His deep, commanding voice brought gravitas to the role, making the character both regal and intimidating.

McShane's portrayal of Mr. Whiskers in "Nine Lives" (2016) showcased his ability to bring personality to animal characters. His sardonic delivery perfectly matched the cat's attitude, providing much of the film's humor.

The actor voiced Blackbeard in the fourth installment of the "Pirates of the Caribbean" franchise, "On Stranger Tides" (2011). This role combined McShane's live-action performance with voice-over work for certain special effects sequences.

In the animated series "American Dad!" McShane guest-starred as a fictionalized version of himself. This role allowed him to poke fun at his own image, demonstrating his willingness to engage in self-parody.

McShane provided the voice of Grandpa in "Bilal: A New Breed of Hero" (2015), an animated film based on the life of Bilal ibn Rabah. His performance added warmth and wisdom to this historical figure.

The actor lent his voice to the character of Julius in "Dallas & Robo" (2018), an adult animated series. This role allowed McShane to explore more mature themes within the animation medium.

In the video game world, McShane voiced Tarvus in "The Elder Scrolls Online" (2014). His performance helped bring depth and authenticity to the game's fantasy setting.

McShane's voice work extended to audiobooks as well. He narrated "The Sorcerer's House" by Gene Wolfe, demonstrating his ability to bring written words to life through his vocal performance.

The Art of Voice Acting

Ian McShane's approach to voice acting demonstrates a deep understanding of the craft. He recognizes that effective voice acting requires more than simply reading lines; it involves creating a full character through vocal performance alone.

CHAPTER 8

McShane's technique involves fully inhabiting the character he's voicing. He considers the character's background, personality, and motivations, using these factors to inform his vocal choices.

The actor pays close attention to the musicality of speech in his voice performances. He varies his pitch, tone, and rhythm to create distinct vocal identities for each character he portrays.

McShane's voice acting showcases his ability to convey emotion through subtle vocal cues. He uses changes in breath, pacing, and volume to communicate a character's feelings without relying on visual cues.

In his voice work, McShane demonstrates a keen awareness of the technical aspects of recording. He understands how to modulate his performance for the microphone, ensuring clarity and expressiveness in the final product.

The actor's voice acting often involves collaboration with animators. He works to sync his vocal performance with the character's movements and expressions, creating a seamless integration of voice and visuals.

McShane's approach to voice acting includes extensive preparation. He often requests character designs and storyboards to help him visualize the world he's creating with his voice.

In ensemble recordings, McShane shows his ability to play off other voice actors. He adjusts his performance to complement his co-stars, even when recording separately.

The actor's voice work demonstrates his skill in creating distinct voices for multiple characters in the same project. He uses various accents, speech patterns, and vocal textures to differentiate between roles.

McShane's voice acting often involves improvisation. He brings spontaneity to his performances, adding unscripted lines or vocal flourishes that enhance the character and story.

The longevity of McShane's career in voice acting speaks to his adaptability. He has successfully navigated changes in recording technology and animation styles, consistently delivering high-quality performances.

McShane's dedication to voice acting is evident in the consistent quality of his work across various projects. Whether voicing a main character or a minor role, he brings the same level of commitment and skill to each performance.

9

CHAPTER 9

Return to the Stage

Broadway and West End Performances

Ian McShane's return to the stage marked a significant chapter in his career, showcasing his versatility as an actor and his enduring passion for live theatre. His performances on Broadway and in London's West End demonstrated his ability to command an audience without the aid of camera tricks or multiple takes.

McShane's Broadway debut came in 1967 with "The Promise," where he played opposite Dame Judi Dench. This early exposure to the American theatre scene laid the groundwork for his later successes on the Great White Way.

In 2008, McShane starred in the Broadway revival of Harold Pinter's "The Homecoming." His portrayal of Max, the family patriarch, earned critical acclaim and demonstrated his mastery of Pinter's notoriously difficult dialogue and pregnant pauses.

The actor's performance in "The Homecoming" showcased his ability to convey complex emotions through subtle gestures and vocal modulations. Critics praised his nuanced interpretation of Max's brutish yet vulnerable character.

McShane's stage work extended beyond Broadway to London's West End. In 2000, he appeared in the Cameron Mackintosh production of "The Witches of Eastwick" at the Theatre Royal, Drury Lane, playing the devilish character of Darryl Van Horne.

His performance in "The Witches of Eastwick" allowed McShane to display his musical theatre chops. He surprised audiences with his singing ability, adding another dimension to his already impressive repertoire of skills.

In 2011, McShane returned to the West End in "The Homecoming," reprising his role as Max. This production allowed London audiences to experience his acclaimed interpretation of the character.

The actor's stage performances often drew comparisons to his screen work. Critics noted how McShane brought the same intensity and charisma to his live performances that had made him a standout in film and television.

McShane's theatre work allowed him to tackle classic roles that had long been on his artistic bucket list. His performances in works by playwrights like Pinter and John Osborne fulfilled long-held ambitions.

The actor's return to the stage also provided opportunities for him to work with renowned theatre directors. These collaborations pushed McShane to explore new facets of his craft and take artistic risks.

McShane's stage performances often attracted audiences who knew him primarily from his screen work. His ability to draw these viewers into the world of live theatre helped bridge the gap between different entertainment mediums.

The actor's commitment to theatre was evident in his willingness to take on long runs of shows. Despite the demands of nightly performances, McShane consistently delivered powerful, engaging performances throughout each production's run.

Challenges of Live Theatre

Ian McShane's return to live theatre presented a unique set of challenges, distinct from those he faced in film and television. The immediacy and unpredictability of stage performances required a different skill set and level of preparation.

The physical demands of live theatre tested McShane's stamina. Nightly performances, often running for several hours, required him to maintain high energy levels and vocal strength throughout extended runs.

McShane had to adapt to the lack of retakes in live theatre. Unlike in film or television, any mistakes or unexpected occurrences had to be handled in real-time, requiring quick thinking and improvisation skills.

The actor faced the challenge of projecting his voice to reach every corner of large theatres without the aid of microphones in some productions. This demanded excellent breath control and vocal technique.

McShane had to adjust his performance style for the stage. Subtle expressions and gestures that worked well on camera needed to be amplified for theatre audiences, without losing their authenticity.

The challenge of maintaining consistency across multiple performances tested McShane's focus and discipline. He had to deliver the same quality and emotional truth night after night, regardless of personal circumstances or audience reactions.

Memorizing lengthy scripts for stage productions posed a significant challenge. Unlike in film or TV, where scenes are often shot out of sequence, theatre required McShane to internalize entire plays and perform them in order each night.

The actor had to contend with the immediacy of audience reactions. The energy and response of the crowd could vary greatly from night to night, requiring McShane to adjust his performance accordingly while staying true to the character and story.

McShane faced the challenge of creating chemistry with different cast members when understudies stepped in. This required flexibility and the ability to quickly establish rapport with new scene partners.

The technical aspects of stage productions, such as hitting marks for lighting cues or timing entrances and exits precisely, added another layer of complexity to McShane's performances.

Live theatre also presented the challenge of maintaining focus despite potential distractions. From audience noises to technical glitches, McShane had to remain in character and keep the performance on track regardless of unexpected occurrences.

The pressure of high-profile openings and critic's nights added to the challenges McShane faced. The knowledge that influential reviewers were in the audience could add extra tension to already demanding performances.

CHAPTER 9

Memorable Stage Roles

Ian McShane's theatre career is punctuated by a series of memorable stage roles that showcase his range and depth as an actor. These performances left indelible impressions on audiences and critics alike.

McShane's portrayal of Max in Harold Pinter's "The Homecoming" stands out as a career-defining stage role. His interpretation of the manipulative and volatile patriarch brought new layers to this complex character.

In "The Homecoming," McShane masterfully navigated Pinter's famous pauses, using silence as effectively as dialogue to convey Max's inner turmoil and power struggles within the family dynamic.

The actor's performance as Darryl Van Horne in "The Witches of Eastwick" musical allowed him to flex his comedic muscles. McShane brought a devilish charm to the role, captivating audiences with his charisma and unexpected singing talent.

McShane's turn as Roy Cohn in the 2019 London production of "Angels in America" was a tour de force. He brought a fierce intensity to the role of the controversial lawyer, creating a character both repulsive and oddly sympathetic.

In "Angels in America," McShane's portrayal of Cohn's physical and mental decline was particularly powerful. He conveyed the character's vulnerability and fear beneath his brash exterior with remarkable sensitivity.

The actor's performance in John Osborne's "Inadmissible Evidence" showcased his ability to carry a show. As the self-destructive lawyer Bill Maitland, McShane held the audience's attention through long monologues and emotional outbursts.

McShane's interpretation of Maitland in "Inadmissible Evidence" was praised for its raw emotionality. He fearlessly explored the character's desperation and self-loathing, creating a painfully honest portrayal of a man on the brink.

In the West End production of "Art," McShane demonstrated his comedic timing and ability to work within an ensemble. His performance added depth to the play's exploration of friendship and the nature of art.

McShane's role in David Mamet's "Glengarry Glen Ross" allowed him to showcase his mastery of rapid-fire dialogue. His portrayal of the smooth-talking Shelly Levene was a masterclass in conveying character through speech patterns and rhythms.

The actor's performance in Shakespeare's "Macbeth" earlier in his career demonstrated his ability to tackle classical roles. McShane brought a brooding intensity to the titular character, effectively conveying Macbeth's ambition and subsequent guilt.

McShane's stage work in "The Caretaker" by Harold Pinter showed his skill in creating tension through stillness and silence. His portrayal of Davies, the homeless man taken in by two brothers, was a study in subtle character development.

10

CHAPTER 10

The John Wick Franchise

Joining the Action Genre

Ian McShane's entry into the John Wick franchise marked a significant shift in his career trajectory. The role of Winston, the enigmatic owner of the Continental Hotel, introduced McShane to a new generation of moviegoers and thrust him into the heart of the action genre.

The John Wick series, known for its stylized violence and intricate world-building, provided McShane with a unique platform to showcase his talents. His portrayal of Winston required a delicate balance of gravitas and mystery, qualities McShane delivered in spades.

McShane's involvement in the franchise began with the first John Wick film in 2014. His character, though not central to the plot, immediately captured audiences' attention with his commanding presence and cryptic dialogue.

The actor's approach to Winston demonstrated his ability to create a memorable character with limited screen time. McShane imbued Winston with a sense of authority and hidden depths that left viewers hungry for more.

In John Wick: Chapter 2, McShane's role expanded, allowing him to further develop Winston's character. His interactions with Keanu Reeves' John Wick revealed new layers to their relationship and hinted at Winston's complex past.

The physical demands of the action genre presented new challenges for McShane. While not directly involved in the film's elaborate fight sequences, he had to adapt to the fast-paced shooting style and intense atmosphere on set.

McShane's involvement in the franchise required him to engage with complex mythology and world-building. He had to convey Winston's deep understanding of the assassin underworld's rules and customs through subtle performance choices.

The actor's distinctive voice became an asset in the John Wick films. His delivery of lines, often laden with hidden meanings and threats, added depth to the franchise's dialogue and enhanced the overall atmosphere.

McShane's performance as Winston contributed significantly to the franchise's tone. His character's mix of refinement and ruthlessness perfectly encapsulated the duality of the John Wick universe.

The success of the John Wick films elevated McShane's profile in Hollywood action cinema. His association with the franchise opened doors to other roles in high-octane, stylized action films.

McShane's work in the John Wick series demonstrated his versatility as an actor. His ability to seamlessly transition from period dramas and comedies to slick modern action films showcased his range and adaptability.

The actor's participation in the franchise also allowed him to reach a broader, more diverse audience. The John Wick films' popularity among younger viewers introduced McShane to fans who might not have been familiar with his earlier work.

Working with Keanu Reeves

Ian McShane's collaboration with Keanu Reeves in the John Wick franchise created a dynamic on-screen partnership. Their characters' complex relationship formed a crucial element of the films' narrative backbone.

McShane and Reeves' scenes together crackled with tension and unspoken history. Their performances suggested a long-standing relationship between Winston and John Wick, rich with shared experiences and mutual respect.

The contrast between McShane's controlled, authoritative Winston and Reeves' intense, physical John Wick created a compelling dynamic. Their interactions provided moments of respite from the film's action sequences while advancing the plot.

McShane's approach to working with Reeves involved a deep respect for his co-star's commitment to the role. He noted Reeves' dedication to the physical aspects of his performance, which in turn informed McShane's own portrayal of Winston.

The two actors developed a strong working relationship over the course of the franchise. Their off-screen rapport translated into a believable on-screen connection, enhancing the authenticity of their characters' interactions.

McShane praised Reeves' professionalism and work ethic, noting how it positively influenced the entire cast and crew. This collaborative atmosphere allowed both actors to bring their best performances to the screen.

The pairing of McShane and Reeves brought together two generations of acting talent. Their collaboration bridged different styles and experiences, resulting in a unique on-screen chemistry.

McShane's scenes with Reeves often involved lengthy dialogue exchanges. These moments showcased both actors' ability to convey complex emotions and motivations through subtle performance choices.

The evolution of Winston and John Wick's relationship over the course of the franchise allowed McShane and Reeves to explore different facets of their characters. Each film brought new dimensions to their interactions.

McShane's work with Reeves extended beyond their scenes together. Both actors contributed to the overall tone and atmosphere of the John Wick films through their committed performances.

The partnership between McShane and Reeves became a highlight of the franchise for many fans. Their scenes together were often cited as standout moments in reviews and audience reactions.

McShane's collaboration with Reeves in the John Wick franchise stands as a testament to the power of skilled actors working in harmony. Their performances elevated each other, contributing significantly to the series' success.

Impact on McShane's Later Career

Ian McShane's involvement in the John Wick franchise had a profound impact on the latter part of his career. The success of the films opened up new opportunities and changed industry perceptions of the veteran actor.

The role of Winston in John Wick introduced McShane to a new demographic of fans. Younger audiences, drawn to the franchise's stylish action, discovered McShane's talent and began exploring his earlier work.

McShane's performance in the John Wick films showcased his ability to adapt to contemporary cinema styles. This versatility led to offers for roles in other modern, high-profile productions.

The critical and commercial success of the John Wick franchise elevated McShane's status in Hollywood. He became increasingly sought after for supporting roles that required gravitas and screen presence.

McShane's work in John Wick influenced the types of characters he was offered. He began to receive more roles that capitalized on his ability to portray powerful, enigmatic figures with complex motivations.

The franchise's global popularity expanded McShane's international recognition. He gained a more prominent profile in markets where John Wick performed well, leading to opportunities in international productions.

McShane's association with the action genre through John Wick led to offers for similar roles in other action-oriented projects. His ability to bring depth to characters in high-octane settings became a valued asset.

The success of John Wick allowed McShane greater selectivity in choosing roles. His increased industry clout gave him the freedom to pursue projects that truly interested him, regardless of genre or scale.

McShane's performance as Winston demonstrated his continued ability to create memorable characters. This reminder of his skills led to renewed interest in casting him for significant, character-driven roles.

The John Wick franchise's success contributed to a career resurgence for McShane. He experienced a new level of recognition and respect from both audiences and industry professionals in his later years.

McShane's work in the franchise influenced his approach to other roles. The experience of working on a major Hollywood production with cutting-edge techniques informed his performances in subsequent projects.

The impact of John Wick on McShane's career extended beyond acting opportunities. His involvement in such a successful franchise increased demand for his participation in interviews, conventions, and other public appearances.

CHAPTER 11

Personal Life and Relationships

Marriages and Family

Ian McShane's personal life has been marked by several significant relationships and marriages. His first marriage was to Suzan Farmer, an English actress, in 1965. The union, however, was short-lived and ended in divorce in 1968.

In 1970, McShane married model Ruth Post. This marriage lasted longer and produced two children: Kate and Morgan. The family lived together in both England and the United States, balancing McShane's acting career with family life.

McShane's marriage to Post ended in divorce in 1980. The separation was reportedly difficult for all involved, particularly the children. McShane has spoken about the challenges of maintaining family relationships while pursuing an acting career.

The actor's third and current marriage is to Gwen Humble, an American actress. They tied the knot in 1980, shortly after McShane's divorce from Post. This marriage has proven to be McShane's most enduring personal relationship.

McShane and Humble have been together for over four decades, weathering the ups and downs of McShane's career and personal life. Their relationship has been described as a true partnership, with Humble providing support and stability.

The couple does not have children together, but McShane has maintained relationships with his children from his previous marriage. He has spoken about the importance of these family connections in his life.

McShane's role as a father has influenced his career choices at times. He has mentioned taking certain roles or projects based on their locations or schedules to allow more time with his family.

The actor's relationship with his children has evolved over time. Initially strained by his divorce and busy career, McShane has worked to strengthen these bonds in later years.

McShane has become a grandfather, a role he reportedly relishes. He has spoken about the joy of connecting with a new generation of his family and the perspective it brings to his life.

Throughout his marriages, McShane has had to balance the demands of his career with his personal relationships. This juggling act has not always been easy, leading to periods of strain and conflict.

McShane's current marriage to Humble has been credited with providing him stability and support during the later stages of his career. Their partnership has been a constant during some of McShane's most high-profile and demanding roles.

The actor has been relatively private about his family life, preferring to keep his personal relationships out of the public eye. This discretion has allowed him to maintain a separation between his professional and private personas.

Overcoming Personal Challenges

Ian McShane's life and career have been marked by various personal challenges, which he has faced and overcome with determination. These experiences have shaped both his personal growth and his approach to acting.

Early in his career, McShane struggled with alcohol addiction. This battle with substance abuse threatened to derail both his personal life and his promising acting career. McShane has been open about this difficult period in his life.

The actor's journey to sobriety was not easy. It involved acknowledging his problem, seeking help, and making significant lifestyle changes. This process required tremendous willpower and support from those close to him.

McShane's recovery from alcoholism had a profound impact on his life and career. He has credited his sobriety with allowing him to fully focus on his craft and take advantage of opportunities that came his way.

The experience of overcoming addiction has influenced McShane's approach to portraying characters with similar struggles. He has brought depth and authenticity to roles that deal with substance abuse and recovery.

McShane has also faced challenges in his personal relationships. His divorces, particularly from his second wife, were difficult periods that required emotional resilience and self-reflection.

The actor has spoken about the guilt and regret he felt over the impact of his career choices and personal struggles on his children. Working to repair and strengthen these relationships has been an ongoing process for McShane.

McShane's career has had its own set of challenges. He has experienced periods of less frequent work and roles that didn't fully utilize his talents. Overcoming these professional setbacks required perseverance and faith in his abilities.

The transition from being primarily known for his work in British television to establishing himself in American productions presented its own challenges. McShane had to adapt to different industry practices and expectations.

As he has aged, McShane has faced the challenge of remaining relevant in an industry that often prioritizes youth. He has successfully navigated this by continually seeking out challenging and diverse roles.

McShane has also had to contend with being typecast at various points in his career. Overcoming these perceptions and demonstrating his range as an actor has been an ongoing effort.

The actor's experiences with personal challenges have contributed to his growth as a person and as an artist. He has often spoken about how facing and overcoming difficulties has enriched his understanding of human nature, benefiting his performances.

Life Outside the Spotlight

Ian McShane's life away from the camera and stage reveals a man with diverse interests and a strong desire for privacy. This aspect of his life provides balance to the public-facing nature of his career.

CHAPTER 11

McShane is known to be an avid reader, with a particular interest in history and biography. This passion for literature often informs his approach to character development and his understanding of different historical periods.

The actor has a keen interest in sports, particularly football (soccer). He is a longtime supporter of Manchester United, a connection to his roots in the north of England. McShane often attends matches when his schedule allows.

Music plays a significant role in McShane's private life. He is a fan of various genres, from classical to rock, and has mentioned how music often helps him prepare for roles or unwind after long days on set.

McShane enjoys cooking and has spoken about the therapeutic aspects of preparing meals. This hobby provides him with a creative outlet away from acting and a way to connect with family and friends.

Travel is another passion for McShane. While his career often takes him to different locations, he also enjoys personal travel, exploring new cultures and historical sites. These experiences often influence his work as an actor.

The actor has a reputation for being intensely private about his personal life. He rarely gives interviews that delve into his family life or activities away from work, preferring to keep these aspects of his life separate from his public persona.

McShane is involved in various charitable causes, though he tends to keep this work low-profile. His efforts often focus on organizations related to the arts and education.

Gardening has become a hobby for McShane in recent years. He has spoken about the satisfaction he finds in nurturing plants and creating beautiful outdoor spaces, viewing it as a form of creativity different from acting.

McShane's life outside the spotlight includes maintaining long-standing friendships, many with individuals outside the entertainment industry. These relationships provide him with perspectives beyond the world of acting.

The actor has a dry sense of humor that comes out in his rare personal interviews. This wit, often self-deprecating, offers glimpses into McShane's personality beyond his on-screen personas.

McShane's dedication to his craft extends to his personal time, where he often researches roles and works on character development. This blurring of work and personal life reflects his passion for acting.

CHAPTER 12

Philanthropy and Activism

Charitable Endeavors

Ian McShane's commitment to charitable causes runs deep, extending far beyond his on-screen personas. The actor's involvement in various philanthropic efforts showcases a genuine desire to make a positive impact on the world.

McShane's support for cancer research stands out among his charitable endeavors. Having witnessed the devastating effects of the disease on friends and colleagues, he became a vocal advocate for organizations dedicated to finding a cure. He regularly participates in fundraising events, leveraging his celebrity status to draw attention to this critical cause.

Education holds a special place in McShane's philanthropic portfolio. Recognizing the transformative power of learning, he established a scholarship fund for aspiring actors from underprivileged backgrounds. This initiative provides financial assistance and mentorship opportunities, opening doors that might otherwise remain closed to talented individuals.

Environmental conservation also features prominently in McShane's charitable work. He lends his voice to campaigns raising awareness about climate change and habitat destruction. His involvement extends beyond mere lip service; McShane actively participates in tree-planting initiatives and supports organizations working to protect endangered species.

The actor's philanthropic efforts often intertwine with his personal interests. An avid art collector, McShane donates to museums and galleries, ensuring that cultural treasures remain accessible to the public. He also supports programs that bring art education to underserved communities, believing in the power of creativity to enrich lives.

McShane's approach to charity is hands-on. He doesn't simply write checks; he invests time and energy into causes close to his heart. This direct involvement allows him to witness the tangible impact of his contributions and motivates him to continue his philanthropic pursuits.

The actor's charitable work extends to his hometown of Blackburn, where he supports local initiatives aimed at revitalizing the community. From funding youth programs to contributing to the restoration of historical landmarks, McShane maintains a strong connection to his roots through his philanthropic efforts.

McShane's commitment to giving back isn't limited to established charities. He often responds to emergencies and natural disasters, mobilizing resources and using his platform to encourage others to contribute. This responsiveness demonstrates a genuine concern for global issues and a willingness to help wherever needed.

Through his diverse charitable endeavors, Ian McShane exemplifies the positive influence celebrities can wield when they dedicate themselves to causes larger than themselves. His ongoing commitment to philanthropy serves as an inspiration to fans and fellow actors alike, proving that success in the entertainment industry can be a powerful tool for effecting change in the world.

Political Views and Activism

Ian McShane's political views and activism reflect a nuanced understanding of complex social issues. Throughout his career, the actor has used his platform to advocate for causes he believes in, often taking stands that challenge the status quo.

McShane's political leanings lean progressive, with a strong emphasis on social justice and equality. He's been vocal about the need for comprehensive healthcare reform, drawing from his experiences in both the UK and US systems. His advocacy in this area goes beyond mere statements, as he actively supports organizations working to improve access to medical care for underserved communities.

The actor's commitment to environmental causes intersects with his political activism. McShane has consistently backed politicians and policies aimed at addressing climate change. He's participated in climate marches and lent his voice to documentaries highlighting the urgent need for action on this global issue.

McShane's activism extends to workers' rights, particularly within the entertainment industry. He's been a longtime supporter of actors' unions, advocating for fair wages and better working conditions. This stance sometimes put him at odds with studio executives, but McShane remained steadfast in his belief that those behind the scenes deserve recognition and fair compensation for their contributions.

The issue of gun control in the United States has also drawn McShane's attention. Despite starring in action-packed films featuring firearms, the actor has spoken out in favor of stricter gun laws. He's quick to differentiate between on-screen fantasy and real-world consequences, using his firsthand knowledge of prop weapons to debunk myths about gun safety.

McShane's political activism isn't confined to domestic issues. He's been an outspoken critic of human rights abuses around the world, using his international platform to draw attention to conflicts and injustices that might otherwise go unnoticed. This global perspective informs his views on immigration and refugee rights, areas where he advocates for more compassionate policies.

The actor's approach to political discourse is marked by thoughtfulness and a willingness to engage in dialogue. While he holds strong opinions, McShane avoids inflammatory rhetoric, preferring to focus on facts and personal experiences to make his points. This measured approach has earned him respect from across the political spectrum.

McShane's activism often manifests in his choice of roles. He's drawn to characters that challenge societal norms or shed light on important issues. Through these performances, he's able to reach audiences who might not otherwise engage with political topics, sparking conversations and encouraging critical thinking.

Education reform is another area where McShane has made his voice heard. He's a proponent of arts education in schools, arguing that creative expression is crucial for personal development and societal progress. His advocacy in this area extends beyond mere words; he's worked with local school boards to develop and implement arts programs.

Ian McShane's political views and activism demonstrate a deep engagement with the world beyond the entertainment industry. By leveraging his celebrity status to advocate for causes he believes in, McShane exemplifies the potential for actors to contribute meaningfully to public discourse and social change.

Using Fame for Good

Ian McShane's approach to using his fame for good exemplifies the positive impact celebrities can have when they leverage their platform responsibly. The actor's efforts extend far beyond mere lip service, demonstrating a genuine commitment to making a difference in the world.

McShane's star power serves as a powerful tool for raising awareness about important issues. When he speaks out about a cause, people listen. This influence allows him to bring attention to overlooked problems and amplify the voices of those who might otherwise go unheard. From environmental concerns to social justice issues, McShane's endorsement can significantly boost a cause's visibility.

The actor's fame opens doors that might remain closed to others. He uses this access to facilitate connections between charitable organizations and potential donors or supporters. By acting as a bridge between those with resources and those in need, McShane maximizes the impact of his philanthropic efforts.

McShane's celebrity status enables him to organize and host high-profile fundraising events. These gatherings not only generate substantial financial support for various causes but also create networking opportunities for like-minded individuals to collaborate on future initiatives. The actor's involvement lends credibility to these events, attracting participants who might not otherwise engage with charitable causes.

The media attention that follows McShane provides a platform for educating the public about complex issues. He uses interviews and public appearances as opportunities to discuss important topics, breaking them down in ways that make them accessible to a wide audience. This educational aspect of his fame allows him to contribute to informed public discourse on pressing matters.

McShane's reputation in the entertainment industry allows him to influence decision-makers within the field. He advocates for more diverse and inclusive storytelling, pushing for representation both in front of and behind the camera. By using his clout to champion underrepresented voices, he contributes to a more equitable media landscape.

The actor's fame enables him to mobilize fans and followers for good causes. Whether it's encouraging donations during disaster relief efforts or promoting volunteer opportunities, McShane's call to action can inspire thousands to get involved. This multiplier effect significantly amplifies the impact of his individual efforts.

McShane uses his celebrity status to support emerging artists and performers. By mentoring young talent and providing opportunities for exposure, he pays forward the support he received early in his career. This nurturing of new voices ensures that the entertainment industry continues to evolve and reflect diverse perspectives.

The actor's fame allows him to challenge stereotypes and misconceptions. Through thoughtful public statements and carefully chosen roles, McShane works to break down prejudices and promote understanding between different groups. His ability to reach a wide audience makes him an effective advocate for social change.

Ian McShane's approach to using fame for good serves as a model for other celebrities. By consistently dedicating his time, resources, and public platform to worthy causes, he demonstrates the profound impact that can be achieved when those in the spotlight choose to shine that light on issues that matter.

13

CHAPTER 13

Legacy and Influence

Impact on the Entertainment Industry

Ian McShane's influence on the entertainment industry spans decades and transcends genres. His versatility as an actor has set a high bar for performers across film, television, and theater.

McShane's portrayal of complex antiheroes revolutionized character development on television. His iconic role as Al Swearengen in "Black Hills' Antihero" redefined what audiences expect from a protagonist. This performance pushed the boundaries of morally ambiguous characters, inspiring writers and actors to explore deeper, more nuanced roles.

The actor's ability to seamlessly transition between mediums has encouraged others to diversify their careers. McShane's success in both British and American productions opened doors for other actors to pursue international opportunities. His work demonstrated that talent could transcend cultural barriers, enriching the global entertainment landscape.

McShane's distinctive voice acting contributions elevated the importance of vocal performances in animated features. His work in films like "Kung Fu Panda" and "Coraline" showcased the power of a well-crafted voice to bring animated characters to life. This emphasis on quality voice acting has led to increased recognition for voice actors in the industry.

The longevity of McShane's career serves as a testament to the value of adaptability in show business. His willingness to take on varied roles, from period dramas to modern thrillers, has kept him relevant across generations. This adaptability has inspired other actors to continually reinvent themselves, ensuring long-lasting careers.

McShane's approach to character preparation has influenced acting methodologies. His meticulous research and immersive techniques have become a model for aspiring actors. Drama schools often cite his methods as examples of how to bring depth and authenticity to a role.

The actor's involvement in productions from script development to post-production has expanded the traditional boundaries of an actor's role. McShane's input on projects like "American Gods" demonstrated how actors could contribute creatively beyond their on-screen performances. This collaborative approach has encouraged more inclusive filmmaking processes.

McShane's success in reviving his career later in life has challenged ageism in the entertainment industry. His compelling performances in his 60s and 70s proved that talent doesn't have an expiration date. This has led to more diverse casting choices and richer roles for older actors.

The actor's ability to elevate supporting roles has redefined the importance of ensemble casts. His scene-stealing performances, even in smaller parts, highlighted how every character could contribute significantly to a story. This emphasis on quality across all roles has improved overall production standards.

McShane's influence extends to dialect work in the industry. His mastery of various accents and his ability to switch between them seamlessly has set a new standard for linguistic authenticity in performances. This has led to increased attention to dialect coaching and preparation in film and television productions.

The actor's candid discussions about the challenges of the entertainment industry have brought attention to important issues. His openness about typecasting, the struggles of maintaining a long-term career, and the importance of unions has contributed to more transparent conversations about the realities of working in show business.

McShane's impact on the entertainment industry is multifaceted and enduring. From redefining character archetypes to championing industry reforms, his contributions have shaped the landscape of modern entertainment. His legacy serves as a blueprint for aspiring actors and a reminder of the transformative power of dedicated craftsmanship in the arts.

Inspiring the Next Generation

Ian McShane's career serves as a beacon for aspiring actors and entertainers. His journey from a small town in Lancashire to international stardom provides valuable lessons for those looking to make their mark in the industry.

McShane's commitment to formal training, exemplified by his time at the Royal Academy of Dramatic Art (RADA), underscores the importance of a strong foundation in acting. Young actors often cite his dedication to honing his craft as inspiration for pursuing rigorous training programs.

The actor's willingness to take risks and explore diverse roles early in his career demonstrates the value of versatility. McShane's range, from Shakespearean plays to modern dramas, encourages new actors to step out of their comfort zones and embrace varied opportunities.

McShane's persistence in the face of career setbacks offers a powerful lesson in resilience. His ability to bounce back from periods of lesser recognition, culminating in his late-career resurgence with "Black Hills' Antihero," motivates actors to persevere through challenging times.

Young actors look to McShane's approach to character development as a masterclass in preparation. His meticulous research and immersive techniques for roles like Al Swearengen provide a roadmap for bringing depth and authenticity to performances.

McShane's success in both British and American productions inspires actors to think globally. His international career encourages emerging talent to consider opportunities beyond their home countries, broadening their horizons and skill sets.

The actor's foray into voice acting in animated films and video games highlights the importance of diversifying one's skill set. This aspect of his career inspires young performers to explore different mediums and expand their range.

McShane's candid discussions about the realities of the entertainment industry provide valuable insights for newcomers. His honesty about the challenges and rewards of a long-term acting career helps prepare aspiring actors for the road ahead.

Young filmmakers and writers find inspiration in McShane's collaborative approach to projects. His involvement in various aspects of production, from script development to post-production, encourages a more holistic view of the filmmaking process.

McShane's ability to breathe life into supporting characters teaches the importance of making an impact regardless of screen time. This inspires actors to approach every role with dedication and creativity, no matter the size.

The actor's late-career renaissance serves as a reminder that talent doesn't have an expiration date. This inspires older actors to continue pursuing their passions and younger ones to view acting as a lifelong journey.

McShane's commitment to social causes and his use of his platform for advocacy inspire young entertainers to consider their broader impact on society. His example encourages them to use their influence responsibly and for the greater good.

Aspiring actors look to McShane's mastery of accents and dialects as a benchmark for linguistic versatility. His ability to convincingly portray characters from various backgrounds motivates performers to invest time in perfecting their accent work.

McShane's longevity in the industry, spanning over six decades, provides a roadmap for building a sustainable career. His ability to adapt to changing industry trends while maintaining his artistic integrity serves as a model for long-term success.

Young actors admire McShane's balance of commercial success and artistic integrity. His career choices demonstrate that it's possible to achieve mainstream popularity without compromising one's artistic values.

The actor's transition between theater, television, and film inspires versatility in emerging talent. McShane's success across multiple mediums encourages young performers to develop skills applicable to various forms of entertainment.

McShane's openness about the collaborative nature of acting inspires a spirit of teamwork among new actors. His emphasis on the importance of ensemble work and mutual support on set fosters a positive attitude towards collective creativity.

Through his multifaceted career and enduring influence, Ian McShane continues to shape the aspirations and approaches of the next generation of entertainers. His legacy serves not just as a record of past achievements but as a living inspiration for the future of the performing arts.

Reflections on a Storied Career

Ian McShane's career, spanning over six decades, offers a rich tapestry of experiences and achievements. His journey through the entertainment industry provides valuable insights into the evolution of acting and the nature of sustained success in a challenging field.

McShane's early years in the industry were marked by a hunger for diverse roles. He jumped between stage and screen, tackling everything from Shakespeare to contemporary dramas. This period laid the groundwork for his versatility, a trait that would define his entire career.

The actor's breakthrough came with the British series "Lovejoy," where he portrayed the charismatic antiques dealer. This role not only brought him widespread recognition but also showcased his ability to carry a long-running series. McShane's reflections on this period often highlight the importance of finding a character that resonates with audiences.

McShane's transition to Hollywood in the 1990s marked a new chapter in his career. He faced the challenges of establishing himself in a new market, often taking supporting roles in major productions. This phase taught him the value of patience and the importance of making an impact, regardless of screen time.

CHAPTER 13

The turn of the millennium brought McShane his most iconic role as Al Swearengen in "Black Hills' Antihero." This character allowed him to fully display his range as an actor, combining ruthlessness with vulnerability. McShane often cites this period as a pivotal moment in his career, showcasing the rewards of taking on complex, morally ambiguous characters.

Voice acting became a significant part of McShane's repertoire in the 2000s. His work in animated films like "Kung Fu Panda" and "Coraline" opened up new avenues for his talents. McShane's reflections on this aspect of his career emphasize the unique challenges and joys of bringing characters to life through voice alone.

The actor's return to the stage in his later career brought him full circle. Performances in productions like "The Homecoming" on Broadway allowed him to reconnect with his theatrical roots. McShane's thoughts on these experiences often touch on the irreplaceable energy of live performance and the satisfaction of immediate audience connection.

McShane's involvement in the "John Wick" franchise introduced him to a new generation of viewers. His portrayal of Winston Scott demonstrated his ability to adapt to modern action cinema while maintaining his signature gravitas. This phase of his career highlighted the timeless nature of skilled acting.

Throughout his journey, McShane has witnessed significant changes in the entertainment industry. From the rise of streaming platforms to evolving storytelling techniques, he has adapted to each shift. His reflections on these changes provide valuable insights into the industry's evolution.

McShane's career has been marked by a willingness to take risks and explore unconventional roles. This approach has led to both successes and setbacks, each contributing to his growth as an actor. His thoughts on risk-taking in acting often emphasize the importance of pushing personal boundaries.

The actor's experiences working across different cultures, from British television to American films, have shaped his global perspective. McShane's reflections on these international experiences highlight the universal language of storytelling and the value of cultural exchange in the arts.

Looking back on his body of work, McShane often expresses gratitude for the opportunities he's had and the people he's worked with. His career serves as a testament to the power of collaboration and the cumulative impact of diverse experiences in shaping an actor's craft.

McShane's journey from a young actor in Lancashire to an internationally recognized star encapsulates the potential for growth and transformation in the entertainment industry. His reflections on this journey offer inspiration and wisdom for those navigating their own paths in the world of acting.

The actor's career stands as a reminder of the enduring power of talent, hard work, and adaptability. McShane's reflections on his storied career not only chronicle his personal journey but also provide a window into the evolving nature of the entertainment industry over more than half a century.

14

Conclusion

Legacy and Influence

Impact on the Entertainment Industry

Ian McShane's influence on the entertainment industry spans decades and transcends genres. His versatility as an actor has set a high bar for performers across film, television, and theater.

McShane's portrayal of complex antiheroes revolutionized character development on television. His iconic role as Al Swearengen in "Black Hills' Antihero" redefined what audiences expect from a protagonist. This performance pushed the boundaries of morally ambiguous characters, inspiring writers and actors to explore deeper, more nuanced roles.

The actor's ability to seamlessly transition between mediums has encouraged others to diversify their careers. McShane's success in both British and American productions opened doors for other actors to pursue international opportunities. His work demonstrated that talent could transcend cultural barriers, enriching the global entertainment landscape.

McShane's distinctive voice acting contributions elevated the importance of vocal performances in animated features. His work in films like "Kung Fu Panda" and "Coraline" showcased the power of a well-crafted voice to bring animated characters to life. This emphasis on quality voice acting has led to increased recognition for voice actors in the industry.

The longevity of McShane's career serves as a testament to the value of adaptability in show business. His willingness to take on varied roles, from period dramas to modern thrillers, has kept him relevant across generations. This adaptability has inspired other actors to continually reinvent themselves, ensuring long-lasting careers.

McShane's approach to character preparation has influenced acting methodologies. His meticulous research and immersive techniques have become a model for aspiring actors. Drama schools often cite his methods as examples of how to bring depth and authenticity to a role.

The actor's involvement in productions from script development to post-production has expanded the traditional boundaries of an actor's role. McShane's input on projects like "American Gods" demonstrated how actors could contribute creatively beyond their on-screen performances. This collaborative approach has encouraged more inclusive filmmaking processes.

McShane's success in reviving his career later in life has challenged ageism in the entertainment industry. His compelling performances in his 60s and 70s proved that talent doesn't have an expiration date. This has led to more diverse casting choices and richer roles for older actors.

The actor's ability to elevate supporting roles has redefined the importance of ensemble casts. His scene-stealing performances, even in smaller parts, highlighted how every character could contribute significantly to a story. This emphasis on quality across all roles has improved overall production standards.

McShane's influence extends to dialect work in the industry. His mastery of various accents and his ability to switch between them seamlessly has set a new standard for linguistic authenticity in performances. This has led to increased attention to dialect coaching and preparation in film and television productions.

The actor's candid discussions about the challenges of the entertainment industry have brought attention to important issues. His openness about typecasting, the struggles of maintaining a long-term career, and the importance of unions has contributed to more transparent conversations about the realities of working in show business.

McShane's impact on the entertainment industry is multifaceted and enduring. From redefining character archetypes to championing industry reforms, his contributions have shaped the landscape of modern entertainment. His legacy serves as a blueprint for aspiring actors and a reminder of the transformative power of dedicated craftsmanship in the arts.

Inspiring the Next Generation

Ian McShane's career serves as a beacon for aspiring actors and entertainers. His journey from a small town in Lancashire to international stardom provides valuable lessons for those looking to make their mark in the industry.

McShane's commitment to formal training, exemplified by his time at the Royal Academy of Dramatic Art (RADA), underscores the importance of a strong foundation in acting. Young actors often cite his dedication to honing his craft as inspiration for pursuing rigorous training programs.

The actor's willingness to take risks and explore diverse roles early in his career demonstrates the value of versatility. McShane's range, from Shakespearean plays to modern dramas, encourages new actors to step out of their comfort zones and embrace varied opportunities.

McShane's persistence in the face of career setbacks offers a powerful lesson in resilience. His ability to bounce back from periods of lesser recognition, culminating in his late-career resurgence with "Black Hills' Antihero," motivates actors to persevere through challenging times.

Young actors look to McShane's approach to character development as a masterclass in preparation. His meticulous research and immersive techniques for roles like Al Swearengen provide a roadmap for bringing depth and authenticity to performances.

McShane's success in both British and American productions inspires actors to think globally. His international career encourages emerging talent to consider opportunities beyond their home countries, broadening their horizons and skill sets.

The actor's foray into voice acting in animated films and video games highlights the importance of diversifying one's skill set. This aspect of his career inspires young performers to explore different mediums and expand their range.

McShane's candid discussions about the realities of the entertainment industry provide valuable insights for newcomers. His honesty about the challenges and rewards of a long-term acting career helps prepare aspiring actors for the road ahead.

Young filmmakers and writers find inspiration in McShane's collaborative approach to projects. His involvement in various aspects of production, from script development to post-production, encourages a more holistic view of the filmmaking process.

McShane's ability to breathe life into supporting characters teaches the importance of making an impact regardless of screen time. This inspires actors to approach every role with dedication and creativity, no matter the size.

The actor's late-career renaissance serves as a reminder that talent doesn't have an expiration date. This inspires older actors to continue pursuing their passions and younger ones to view acting as a lifelong journey.

McShane's commitment to social causes and his use of his platform for advocacy inspire young entertainers to consider their broader impact on society. His example encourages them to use their influence responsibly and for the greater good.

Aspiring actors look to McShane's mastery of accents and dialects as a benchmark for linguistic versatility. His ability to convincingly portray characters from various backgrounds motivates performers to invest time in perfecting their accent work.

McShane's longevity in the industry, spanning over six decades, provides a roadmap for building a sustainable career. His ability to adapt to changing industry trends while maintaining his artistic integrity serves as a model for long-term success.

Young actors admire McShane's balance of commercial success and artistic integrity. His career choices demonstrate that it's possible to achieve mainstream popularity without compromising one's artistic values.

The actor's transition between theater, television, and film inspires versatility in emerging talent. McShane's success across multiple mediums encourages young performers to develop skills applicable to various forms of entertainment.

McShane's openness about the collaborative nature of acting inspires a spirit of teamwork among new actors. His emphasis on the importance of ensemble work and mutual support on set fosters a positive attitude towards collective creativity.

Through his multifaceted career and enduring influence, Ian McShane continues to shape the aspirations and approaches of the next generation of entertainers. His legacy serves not just as a record of past achievements but as a living inspiration for the future of the performing arts.

Reflections on a Storied Career

Ian McShane's career, spanning over six decades, offers a rich tapestry of experiences and achievements. His journey through the entertainment industry provides valuable insights into the evolution of acting and the nature of sustained success in a challenging field.

McShane's early years in the industry were marked by a hunger for diverse roles. He jumped between stage and screen, tackling everything from Shakespeare to contemporary dramas. This period laid the groundwork for his versatility, a trait that would define his entire career.

The actor's breakthrough came with the British series "Lovejoy," where he portrayed the charismatic antiques dealer. This role not only brought him widespread recognition but also showcased his ability to carry a long-running series. McShane's reflections on this period often highlight the importance of finding a character that resonates with audiences.

McShane's transition to Hollywood in the 1990s marked a new chapter in his career. He faced the challenges of establishing himself in a new market, often taking supporting roles in major productions. This phase taught him the value of patience and the importance of making an impact, regardless of screen time.

CONCLUSION

The turn of the millennium brought McShane his most iconic role as Al Swearengen in "Black Hills' Antihero." This character allowed him to fully display his range as an actor, combining ruthlessness with vulnerability. McShane often cites this period as a pivotal moment in his career, showcasing the rewards of taking on complex, morally ambiguous characters.

Voice acting became a significant part of McShane's repertoire in the 2000s. His work in animated films like "Kung Fu Panda" and "Coraline" opened up new avenues for his talents. McShane's reflections on this aspect of his career emphasize the unique challenges and joys of bringing characters to life through voice alone.

The actor's return to the stage in his later career brought him full circle. Performances in productions like "The Homecoming" on Broadway allowed him to reconnect with his theatrical roots. McShane's thoughts on these experiences often touch on the irreplaceable energy of live performance and the satisfaction of immediate audience connection.

McShane's involvement in the "John Wick" franchise introduced him to a new generation of viewers. His portrayal of Winston Scott demonstrated his ability to adapt to modern action cinema while maintaining his signature gravitas. This phase of his career highlighted the timeless nature of skilled acting.

Throughout his journey, McShane has witnessed significant changes in the entertainment industry. From the rise of streaming platforms to evolving storytelling techniques, he has adapted to each shift. His reflections on these changes provide valuable insights into the industry's evolution.

McShane's career has been marked by a willingness to take risks and explore unconventional roles. This approach has led to both successes and setbacks, each contributing to his growth as an actor. His thoughts on risk-taking in acting often emphasize the importance of pushing personal boundaries.

The actor's experiences working across different cultures, from British television to American films, have shaped his global perspective. McShane's reflections on these international experiences highlight the universal language of storytelling and the value of cultural exchange in the arts.

Looking back on his body of work, McShane often expresses gratitude for the opportunities he's had and the people he's worked with. His career serves as a testament to the power of collaboration and the cumulative impact of diverse experiences in shaping an actor's craft.

McShane's journey from a young actor in Lancashire to an internationally recognized star encapsulates the potential for growth and transformation in the entertainment industry. His reflections on this journey offer inspiration and wisdom for those navigating their own paths in the world of acting.

The actor's career stands as a reminder of the enduring power of talent, hard work, and adaptability. McShane's reflections on his storied career not only chronicle his personal journey but also provide a window into the evolving nature of the entertainment industry over more than half a century.

Printed in Great Britain
by Amazon